FREEDOM FROM UNHEALTHY RELATIONSHIPS

The Secrets to Building Strong and Lasting Bonds, Resolve Conflicts, Improve Intimacy and Overcome Codependency.

Joseph Ajayi

FREEDOM FROM UNHEALTHY RELATIONSHIPS

Cover Design - Starline on Freepik[1] and Syldavia on Istockphoto[2]

---

1. Image by Starline: www.freepik.com
2. Stock photo by Syldavia: www.istockphoto.com

Contents

Introduction

> Don't settle for a relationship that won't let you be yourself.
>
> — Oprah Winfrey, an American T.V. Host

In this materialistic and fast-moving world, we often don't realize that our lives are one of the biggest blessings of God that cannot be measured on any scale. Life is a beautiful journey that perfectly blends ups and downs, happiness and sorrow, and goodness and evil, making it phenomenal. Apart from this, there are essential elements without which our lives will be incomplete, and those are the most treasured relationships we live and cherish. These different relationships teach us exciting ways to survive the roller coaster ride of life and help us develop our perspectives, emotions, and behaviors toward the people and the world around us.

In life, we are blessed with many relationships, out of which a few always vow to stand beside us like our eternal blood relatives; such relationships must be nourished with love, respect, and compassion to flourish, like our friends, colleagues, and most importantly—our life partner or spouse. For instance, when two people with many dissimilarities come together in a married relationship, they discover many unsaid and unexplored things about each other and their relationship, making life's journey a new expedition. Many times, in this attempt, knowingly or unknowingly, one hurts or triggers the weak point of the other, thus giving rise to arguments, heated conversations, and conflicts. When these unfriendly exchanges don't end, or either of the partners quits the discussion, the situation worsens, leading to misunderstandings and unsaid grudges. Slowly and steadily, these unpleasant things, when not adequately addressed, bring the relationship to a point that marks the beginning of toxicity, with episodes of verbal abuse, physical assault, and mental torture.

Living a happy marital life is not a matter of competition or a win-lose game for the couple but a matter of pride to continue this challenging relationship by going against all the odds. However, not all married relationships end on such a happy note, and they often become targets of domestic violence, creating loads of difficulties for both the partners and others associated with them. As a matter of fact, it requires lots of courage, patience, wisdom, and resilience to handle the atrocities and trauma of an unhealthy relationship, which either makes one very strong to revolt against their partner or compels them to surrender before compromising and enduring all the pain and agony of life. Sometimes, when the situation exceeds a respectable limit, crossing all boundaries leads to the ultimate separation or divorce.

Hence, *Freedom from unhealthy relationships* is a comprehensive guide that reveals the secrets of building a strong and lasting relationship by resolving conflicts, improving intimacy, and overcoming codependency. The book is the best read for all those who are either a victim of unhealthy relationships or have ever experienced toxicity in their past relationships and need to heal and regain their peace or for new dates who intend to know how to avoid unhealthy relationships. It focuses on imparting complete knowledge about the different types of unhealthy relationships in our society and the simple markers that can help differentiate between healthy and toxic relationships. Moreover, the book highlights all the probable causes and early warning signs of toxicity that can help one rate their married life and take the necessary steps to save their relationship at the right time.

It covered an exciting aspect of married life, which is codependency, and explains how it acts as a slow poison for a healthy relationship. It shows the impacts of mental health conditions on relationships. Apart from this, the book's versatility lay in the empowering content that shared interesting tips to heal broken relationships and help combat divorce as much as practicable. It reveals steps to take if a relationship is discontinued and efforts to find peace and start all over. Overall, the book is a true gem for readers who seek strength, power, and guts to heal and mend their broken relationship with love, compassion, and patience, making their relationship eternal. At this point, there are various mind-boggling questions, like:

- Is my relationship with my partner toxic?
- What should I do to save my relationship from becoming toxic?
- Is opting for divorce a feasible choice for me?
- Can I live a happy life after divorce?

Freedom from Unhealthy Relationships is not just a guide; it's your beacon, illuminating the path to discover and sidestep toxic relationships even before you utter 'I do.' This transformative guide will empower the married to thwart habits and attitudes that poison unions. It extends a lifeline to those trapped in toxicity, guiding them to reclaim their lives and rediscover happiness. Unlock the wisdom within these pages; let it be the key to your freedom from unhealthy relationships. Each chapter ends with the required action steps to implement the lessons gleaned.

Get ready to embark on a journey to freedom – a freedom that comes from within, paving the way for a life untethered from toxic ties. Your transformation begins now. *"You will know the truth and the truth will make you free"* [1]

---

1. *John 8:32*

Chapter 1

Knowing an Unhealthy Relationship

> *Don't light yourself on fire trying to brighten someone else's existence.*
>
> — *Charlotte Eriksson, an Eminent Author*

Every being, whether a man or a woman, deserves joy, satisfaction, and security by enjoying the perks of a healthy relationship. For ages, people from different places and cultures have followed the tradition of uniting two people into a wedding knot as a religious act of procreation. As is often said and believed, marriages are made in heaven. Almost every married couple dreams of having a peaceful and happy life ever after. But, many times, the uncertainties of life bring us to such a pathway where we can't even decide what to do or how to respond to the situation that crops up before us. As God has created all of us from the dust of the ground, none of us are perfect in any sphere of our lives. Thus, it is very typical for us to commit mistakes, which often become the prime reason for the challenges and pains in a relationship that eventually put us through various ordeals. So, let's understand the value of a happy and healthy relationship by comprehensively construing the exact picture of an unhealthy relationship.

Healthy Relationship vs Unhealthy Relationship

A marital relationship exhibits various colors and emotions among all the relationships we are blessed with in our lives. Every little thing is essential in defining the type of relationship one lives in. A husband and a wife are like the two wheels of a cart, and it is sometimes impossible to maintain a perfect balance and harmony in life without the cooperation and efforts of either of them. Moreover, various elements in a relationship, like trust, respect, love, and compassion, genuinely govern the quality of one's life. As everyone is different and holds a unique set of emotions, attitudes, thought processes, behavioral patterns, and desires, we see myriad relationships blooming around us in the silhouette of nuptials.

Apparently, it is not a cakewalk to maintain a healthy relationship in wedlock, as many ups and downs make the journey a roller coaster ride. It requires a genuine and adequate commitment to make a relationship last long. It is expected to have differences in opinions and personal interests among couples, which can result in clashes and arguments. However, such conflicts don't mean that there is no love or a lack of compatibility in a relationship. A healthy relationship supports the growth and development of both individuals by providing the required space, liberty, and honor to express themselves and be their true selves. Unlikely, in an unhealthy relationship, the partners don't share a friendly tie but instead display a competitive attitude accompanied by various negative feelings like jealousy, hatred, or mistrust. In extreme cases, either of the partners ends up becoming the victim of verbal abuse, mental distress, physical torture, and, at times, even sexual harassment.

Living and carrying on a happy and fruitful married life demands a great sense of accountability; otherwise, it may result in harmful competition with the partner, which can probably be a blame game, making one's life miserable. Apart from this, one has to exhibit an excellent level of adaptability by listening to and accepting the thought processes and suggestions of one's spouse. At every step of a marriage, many challenging situations require the nerve of steel to handle and overcome them. It is effortless to spoil a relationship, but it takes years to create love and compatibility with each other to create a pleasant and flourishing atmosphere that can be a stepping stone in the journey of making a happy family. Ending a relationship and running away from life's problems is not the ultimate freedom; instead, one needs to gather all one's strength and wit to make a wise decision by considering all the aspects of life to enjoy the desired relationship. So, keeping one's ego and agony aside, it is necessary to think about the mental health condition, social behavior, and attitude of your partner before deciding whether your relationship is healthy or unhealthy.

Unhealthy Relationship vs Toxic Relationship

In life, we always strive and expect the best for ourselves in every aspect, but we never know what lies ahead. Often, our destiny brings us to a situation where it is all up to us to decide what is best for us. Sometimes, our inborn qualities, behaviors, and attitudes save us from becoming prey to something unpleasant. Still, at other times, these traits can only become a reason for our pain and destruction. When talking about married relationships, we need to clearly know and understand that there is a fine line between an unhealthy relationship and a toxic one. When two different individuals come together, it is very logical for them to have differences in opinions, thoughts, and ideas. Many times, despite being aware and educated about different easy and friendly ways to communicate with a partner, people opt for complex and harsh behavior. Every marriage generally begins on a positive and happy note, but the scenario doesn't remain the same for life. Numerous unseen reasons crop up as one tries to adjust and compromise in wedlock, making one's life a challenge.

While we look around us, we may find many couples who never plan a date night, go out to shop with each other, attend family functions, or watch movies together. But this does not make their relationship toxic, as there can be many possible reasons and explanations for such unusual behavior. However, if this act is mutual and the couple understands each other, they will never end up arguing or fighting over all this stuff. Many times, problems on the professional front and various other family pressures may preoccupy an individual's mind, creating negativity within them. These negativities get further aggravated by the indifferent behavior of the spouse, which eventually triggers the bad wolf within. The bad wolf refers to all the unwanted negative emotions and feelings that hover in one's mind, making one vulnerable and violent. All this compels an individual to exhibit the worst side of their personality by indulging in verbal abuse and physical violence with their partner. With the commencement of any such unjust, violent act, a married relationship enters the category of a toxic relationship, which evidently differentiates it from an unhealthy relationship.

Types of Unhealthy Relationships

Not all married relationships always start with abuse or violent activities; many of them never enter an abusive phase. However, the harsh truth of life is that a few of these heavenly relationships do suffer the hardships of domestic violence. Looking out for a fantastic partner who attracts you with their charm and treats you in the right way is not always a dream come true for all. Instead, it is more of a fantasized reality for many, as the red flags and flaws of your married partners make you witness an inescapable nightmare. Falling in love and joining in holy matrimony with the person of your choosing is truly a divine gift, even though, at times, one may inadvertently overlook the more profound meaning hidden beneath the disarray of life's challenges and imperfections.

The initial days of marriage are full of love and passion to explore one another, which fills the days with excitement and exhilaration. However, a happy start may differ for many, except if the right decisions and compromises are in place. Sometimes, being in a married relationship may seem burdensome, overwhelming, and more like an arduous task, which marks the beginning of an unhealthy marriage. Often, marriage can be perceived as a gift box that provides immense pleasure when you get it in your hand while unaware of what it may carry. Similarly, sometimes you may end up in an unhealthy or toxic relationship that slowly and gradually deteriorates you from within, just like a termite eats away a log of wood.

Research reveals that at least one out of every four women and one in every ten men are victims of intimate partner physical violence in their entire lifetime (Cherry, 2018). While explicitly talking about the United States, around twenty people experience physical abuse by their partners every minute, which approximates to about 15% of intimate partner physical and emotional abuse (Cherry, 2018). Having knowledge and insight about the various types of unhealthy relationships is crucial to help one identify and unveil the puzzled behaviors of their partner, which can help in taking the proper steps to protect oneself from a severe emotional breakdown. So, let's explore the varied levels of unfriendliness in a married relationship that can quickly help you differentiate between unhealthy and toxic relationships.

Stagnant Relationship

Each relationship has different phases and keeps changing with time, especially the bonding between the couples, which witnesses a wide range of transitioning emotions with the passing years. Sometimes, the love, passion, and excitement to be with your partner begin to die down as time progresses. In this dull and depressing phase of one's love life, you may feel like nothing is working to reignite the spark between you and your spouse. Being stuck in the whirl of a stagnant relationship feels like you have no space left for two-way communication and romance; one feels a lack of trust and understanding, which often results in fights. This type of relationship can drain you both physically and emotionally, as you think that there is no love or connection with your spouse anymore. Being in a stagnant relationship could make you feel like nothing is going as planned and everything seems to be on the verge of despair. Many simple reasons can drift among the couples, like being preoccupied with the daily chores, the inability to balance personal and professional life, a lack of connection, miscommunication, no growth, fixed mindsets, and mismatched lifestyles and values.

Carefree Relationship

A marriage is said to be successful when two different people come together to share their thoughts, emotions, and responsibilities with a promise to stand firm with each other in all phases of life. We all have many expectations from our partners, but sometimes, when they fail to live up to those expectations, it may create issues. Especially being with someone who seems to show little concern for anything can feel quite burdensome. When your partner is negligent about your expectations, priorities, and dreams, it may burden the relationship. In a carefree relationship, the partner is reluctant to adjust according to the hopes and will of their spouse, which gradually worsens the scenario. However, marriage is about coping with situations by consistently learning, accepting, and tolerating the weaknesses of your soulmate. But when the efforts are only from one side, and the other partner is carefree about every little thing, it begins to detach the feelings, causing a drift between them. However, unlike other toxic relationships, there is always scope to get things back to normal by talking about the differences with each other, offering help and support, changing one's attitude, or proactively finding a solution for the stubborn attitude by seeking help from a counselor.

Competitive Relationship

Marriage is not just a contract to live and share; instead, it is more like an amazing game of life in which you and your spouse are the real teammates who work for the progress and betterment of each other, supporting each other through the thick and thin of life. In married life, nothing is called mine or yours; it is simply 'us.' However, sometimes, some couples cannot work together as a team and often compete with one another. A competitive relationship begins with either of the two partners showing competitiveness, eventually exhibiting the same behavior on both ends. Insecurity is the biggest culprit in these relationships, which ultimately builds up lots of jealousy, secretive habits, finding pleasure in the pain of one another, and looking for instances to put down their partners. A competitive relationship usually begins with a concealed phase, where the gestures of the insecure partner are not visible. Still, gradually, they build up to the point where their impacts are hurtful and evident. A competitive relationship has envy, which is often the beginning stage of ending up in a hostile or resentful relationship. When extreme levels are crossed, this type of relationship can also end up in toxicity, like an abusive relationship where one partner tries to manipulate and control the other out of jealousy, insecurity, and unhealthy competition between them.

Sociopath Relationship

Getting into a relationship with a sociopath may or may not be toxic, but if it is, then it does cause immense pain and emotional trauma. A sociopath is mostly the self-obsessed one who lacks empathy for their partners, is manipulative for their benefit, hardly shows up in need of others, and exhibits no guilt, shame, or remorse after hurting others. Being in a lifelong and pious relationship after marrying a sociopath can harm your peace of mind and mental health. Some of the common signs that can help you identify if your soulmate is a sociopath is arrogant behavior, a superficial charming attitude, pathological lying, impulsive behaviors, never following the rules, which can end up in violence or hurting others, and using abusive and guilt-trip tricks to change the game. Being in a sociopath relationship can have harsh impacts on your mental as well as physical health, as it may cause mental illness, stress, and trauma, let you lose control over your temperament, disable you from concentrating on work life, and, in extreme cases, isolate you from family and close friends. Even if your sociopath partner is not exhibiting violent or abusive behaviors, it is still not easy to spend your entire life with them. Sociopaths have no control over themselves and thus portray a spectrum of behaviors that confuse and drain you mentally. Therefore, when a relationship with someone who exhibits sociopathic traits becomes detrimental to your well-being, it is crucial to seek help, as nothing should take precedence over your health and overall wellness.

Narcissistic Relationship

Being in a relationship with a narcissistic partner can make you feel alone, uncared for, and unheard. In the initial days of your relationship, a narcissist would show healthy emotions and feelings like kindness, compassion, and love. However, as time passes, your narcissistic soulmate begins to reveal their true color and exhibit rude, manipulative, and abusive behavior. An uncontrolled narcissistic behavior of a spouse may result in the breakdown of the partner's self-confidence, self-worth, and self-esteem, as their repeated behaviors of gaslighting, criticism, and rageful reactions could damage one's self-image. Striving in such a negative relationship can be emotionally draining, incredibly exhausting, and challenging to handle. Some of the common signs that can help one identify a narcissistic partner are: they are more interested in self-talk, give preferences to themselves, show less or no concern for their soulmates, are manipulative, are oversensitive to criticism, and are always in need of compliments from others as well as their partners. Many simple ways can help one face the situation without doubting oneself. For instance, practicing self-care, exploring yourself, setting healthy boundaries, and giving up unrealistic expectations from your narcissistic partner can possibly help you cope with the worst scenarios.

Resentful Relationship

Sometimes, being maltreated may initiate a nagging behavior that hovers over one's mind, swinging between feelings of disappointment and anger. Every relationship starts on a happy note; however, gradually, both partners may begin to have conflict over the little things in life, like having different opinions about things, unmatched goals and expectations, or different life priorities. These conflicting thoughts tend to pile up in one's mind and create a perception of not being treated the right way, which eventually causes resentment. In a resentful relationship, it is challenging for partners to share genuine feelings of care, kindness, compassion, empathy, trust, and honesty toward each other. Instead, these feelings are replaced by jealousy, anger, ill-will, frustration, and bitterness toward each other. In most cases, being in such a toxic relationship becomes a demanding task that may drain your positivity, confidence, and enthusiasm for living life to the fullest. Some of the most common signs of identifying if you are feeling resentment in your relationship are a consistent feeling of disappointment and anger toward your partner, a lack of empathy, reduced intimacy, frequent complaining about your spouse, using sarcastic remarks, feeling agitated, and wanting to escape from this burdening relationship.

Abusive Relationship

Identifying the abuse and dealing with it can be a challenging task. Abuse of any kind is damaging and hurtful, physical or emotional. Emotionally abusive relationships are more sophisticated and are like a toxic mind game that eventually drains the partner's energy, peace of mind, and courage to navigate through depressing situations. If your partner displays an unpredictable flow of emotions and affection, then you are living in an abusive relationship. It's not essential that in an abusive relationship, both partners are equally involved in creating issues and toxicity. Sometimes, it can be the one who figures out the probable ways to manipulate their spouse or the situation until it worsens. It is difficult to guess about abusive relationships from the outside, as in most cases, everything looks normal and perfect to the other people around. One common trait of an abusive partner is that they try to make things look normal to their spouse to clarify and justify their acts, for they believe they are normal and not harmful. In such cases, it is pretty demanding for the victim to understand if they are living in a toxic relationship. In a healthy relationship, the couples have conflicts that are then solved through arguments, debates, and the sharing of opinions by both partners. However, in an abusive relationship, one partner tries to take control of the thoughts, actions, and feelings of their spouse using several manipulative tricks like isolating them from their family and close friends, taking over financial management, emotional blackmail, guilt trips, and coercion. It is very challenging being in an abusive relationship.

Violent Relationship

Every relationship, even the strongest and healthier ones, has some conflict, argument, or disagreement over specific topics at some point in time. However, using any violent activity to threaten your partner is not normal; instead, it is an act of relationship violence, which is wrong. Sometimes, either of the partners tries to use improper gestures and acts of violence to create terror over their spouse and develop power and control over them. A violent relationship can be anything from physical torture to emotional abuse, sexual harassment, and verbal or financial abuse. Apart from the physical abuse that includes hitting, slapping, choking, and punching a violent partner can also try to force you to do any sexual act like kissing, touching, or marital rape without your consent.

Furthermore, preventing one from using money or contacting their family and friends is another form of a violent relationship. A violent relationship is the extreme form of an unhealthy relationship between couples. Living in a toxic relationship like this one can take a toll on your emotional, physical, and psychological well-being, impacting your life drastically; therefore, staying away from a violent relationship becomes an urgent need of the hour. Nevertheless, various obstacles, such as the presence of young children, societal expectations, limited financial and family support, and personal insecurities and apprehensions, can fasten the burdensome chains that hinder individuals from extricating themselves from such a relationship.

Required Action Steps

1. It is a must for every individual in a relationship to know and understand the difference between a healthy and a toxic relationship.
2. One must be mindful of the fine line that distinguishes an unhealthy relationship from a toxic relationship, as it can help one manage their relationships better.
3. After knowing about the status of one's relationship, one must take immediate steps to mend the relationship before it gets too late.
4. Performing reflective activities and interacting with the partner can help one analyze the level of toxicity in their relationship.
5. Adopting a passive approach and expecting destiny to steer your relationship is unwise, for it is said, "God will not do what He can do until we do what we should do."

Life is inherently unpredictable and can present various challenging situations within relationships. Therefore, maintaining mental readiness for both the highs and lows and seeking appropriate help is a fundamental principle one should uphold to navigate life's twists and turns with grace and minimize chaos. Remember the word of the Messiah, *"In me you may have peace, in the world you will have tribulation, but be of good cheer, I have overcome the world."* [1]

---

1. *John 16:33*

Chapter 2

Causes That Lead to Unhealthy Relationships

> *Ego is probably one of the biggest poisons we can have - it's toxic to any environment.*
>
> — *Jonny Kim, an American Physician*

In the race of our busy lives, we often forget that running a healthy married life demands the consistent efforts, commitments, and willingness of both partners, which can help you flourish and be at your best by becoming a solid support system for each other. However, when either of the soulmates becomes ignorant, portrays toxic and ruthless behavior, practices unhealthy coping mechanisms, or develops pessimistic thoughts, it disrupts the entire relationship. A married relationship is never made to be toxic, as it is an empowering bond among the couples that inculcates the zeal and enthusiasm to live life to the fullest. This beautiful relationship can improve mental and physical health, boost stress-coping abilities, and many more positive things that can contribute to a happy and healthy life. Yet sometimes, we make a choice and fall for an individual who is either struggling to heal from their dysfunction, is trying to fight against their negative mindset, or is a victim of depression; this can be the turning point of your happy life, as it may mark the beginning of an unhealthy relationship. So, it is necessary for a couple to know the alarming reasons that can be a significant threat to their budding married life.

Factors That Trigger Toxicity in a Relationship

As we have already explored, unhealthy relationships are pretty common and have different levels of atrocities and trauma associated with them. In the worst situation, a toxic relationship ultimately compels one to move toward separation or divorce, as people think that this is the only way out to find peace of mind and build up one's self-confidence once again. So, let's delve deep and explore the crucial factors transforming a smooth-running relationship into a toxic one.

Work Priorities

No doubt life is a race in which each of us struggles to achieve the best in our personal lives and on the professional front. To maintain a successful career and lifestyle, one must often remember to prioritize their relationships, especially their married life. The bond between married couples is like a blooming flower that demands daily nourishment to revive it and keep it as fresh as it was in the initial phases. However, being negligent and unable to maintain the right balance between professional and personal life will slowly and steadily hamper our precious relationships. When you bring your office life home, it wastes your valuable time and leaves no room to talk peacefully with your spouse. All this creates misunderstandings, increases conflicts, triggers heated arguments and differences of opinion, and raises many more complex issues between a couple. The seeds of an unhealthy relationship are often unknowingly sown due to the mismanagement of time and failure to prioritize our married life goals, which eventually give birth to an extreme situation and toxicity in our married relationship. Hence, one must deliberate to ensure adequate boundaries between workspace and home space; this will go a long way to reduce the relationship's toxicity burden.

Unmet Desires

Each one of us has several desires and hidden fantasies related to our married life, like feeling loved, valued, safe, respected, and sexually satisfied. Often preoccupied in the hurly-burly of life, one fails to satisfy their partner's desires and basic needs. Gradually, the unmet needs give rise to negative feelings like losing patience, frustration, and extreme anger, which begin to show up and hamper the relationship between a husband and wife. In such situations, one may often behave in an emotionally abusive manner and may force their partner to fulfill their unmet desires and needs. This act of toxicity to satisfy oneself can be anything ranging from making your soulmate cry to making yourself feel valued and loved to sometimes even forcing oneself against their will to gain sexual satisfaction. To get rid of the frustrations of these kinds of unmet needs, a person usually ends up indulging in violent, abusive, and hurtful activities with their partner, which is enough to shed the threads of the delicate relationship.

Past Trauma

Feeling stress is an integral part of life. Life is full of instances that can cause worry or frustration, but most of the time, family support and the skills within us help us get through challenging situations. But in several circumstances, the stress level or the trauma of an unwanted happening is so great, and it lasts for so long that it overwhelms the coping ability of an individual. Similarly, the trauma of dealing with toxic stress like physical or emotional violence can leave behind a dark impression and scars on one's heart and soul, which may interfere with one's future life and make one vulnerable to risky behaviors and mental health issues. Being in a relationship with someone who has had previous disturbing life experiences may increase the chances of getting into a toxic relationship. The experience of life is like the dark shadows that follow one everywhere. Likewise, a person who has had a toxic relationship in the past believes that being violent and abusive is normal behavior and continues doing the same, ruining their present married life too.

Clashing Future Interests

Marriage is a relationship in which two people from different cultures, places, and family backgrounds come together to start a beautiful life. However, sometimes, when two people from totally different backgrounds have varied dreams, aspirations, and unmatched goals for life, it may create conflict between them. For instance, in some cases, if a husband is willing to start a family and have kids, but the wife is more inclined toward gaining stability in their professional life, it may become a matter of conflict. In a married relationship, a man often expects his wife to support the family if he is financially weak. In such cases, if one is unwilling to take the financial burden over her shoulders, it becomes a clash. These are just a few examples, but many different scenarios can crop up in a married relationship and ultimately become a matter of conflict between the couple, which often makes the relationship complex and unhealthy.

Incompatible Marriage

There is often a significant age difference between married couples due to many dissimilarities in their thoughts and emotions. The differences, like lack of maturity level and varied life preferences, give rise to incompatibility in marriage. Another primary reason for incompatibility is the inability of either spouse to devote themselves to the married relationship fully. In some cases, when family members have an immense influence on the minds of either of the partners, it results in grudges between the two, resulting in arguments, misunderstandings, and conflicts in most cases. Apart from this, sometimes couples tied up in the bonds of marriage merely because of social pressure may be compelled to live that relationship willingly or unwillingly, thus making it challenging to form compatibility between the two. However, incompatible relationships are more susceptible to toxicity and violence, as either of the spouses may be adamant about transforming their other half as an extension of themselves while forcing them to change their behaviors, thus initiating emotional abuse or manipulation. Two can not walk together unless they agree.[1]

Physical Abuse

In married life, there is a very fine line between couples called dignity, which defines their boundaries. Once this line is broken, the partners enter the abusive and violent phase of the relationship, which may include physical torture, mental abuse, and sexual harassment. The relationship then takes a toxic turn and becomes very difficult to retrieve. Restarting a happy life after this is quite challenging, and it will require divine intervention because of the scars and traumas of these physical assaults, which haunt one again and again like a nightmare, making one's life bitter, depleted, and unvalued. Many times, not all toxic relationships are abusive as they do not involve any physical torture; however, all abusive relationships are toxic as they drastically impact one's mindset and change one's entire perception of marriage and one's significant other. Once your relationship enters an abusive phase, it is quite challenging for the partners to get over the happenings and other repercussions. More often, an abusive relationship follows a regular cycle that includes four phases: tension building, abusive behaviors, seeking forgiveness from the victim, peaceful days—and the cycle repeating.

Infidelity

Infidelity is complicated; not only can it destroy your married life, but it can also shatter your hopes and ability to trust anyone else in the future, ruin the lives of your kids, and have a drastic psychological impact, causing anxiety, depression, and stress. However, apart from all of this, cheating on your partner can turn your current relationship into a toxic one, eventually eroding your peace of mind and deteriorating your physical and mental health. Infidelity is morally and spiritually wrong, hurtful, and a violation of someone's trust and loyalty. Some of the reasons that initiate this kind of relationship are but not limited to lack of fear of God, a lack of bonding and understanding with your spouse, not being sexually satisfied, unhappiness in married life, or physical affairs. Often, in such a situation, it is expected that the couple's peace in their married life is depleted. Being cheated on or cheating on your partner can initiate a chain of changed behaviors and emotions, causing arguments, showing a carefree attitude, and a lack of interest in one's spouse. In other cases, if the partner's infidelity is revealed, it may ignite an outburst of mixed emotions like angry arguments, extreme anguish, hatred, emotional instability, fear of being left, pain, and intense sadness. All these factors contribute toward worsening the situation and may create drift among the couples, which causes a toxic relationship.

Communication Gap

Every person has a different perspective on the importance of communication in a relationship. It may be one of the key elements to developing a successful and healthy relationship. Lack of communication is one of the major causes of conflict in relationships as it increases the chances of having arguments, misunderstandings, suspicions, lying, spying, and even violence. Not being able to communicate your feelings with your spouse can cause stress and anxiety, which also ignites the trust issue between couples. The most probable cause of a communication breakdown is that either both partners have stopped discussing essential issues or cannot have regular talks without having any conflict or arguments. In both cases, couples firmly believe initiating communication can turn into heated quarrels and a never-ending clash. The consistent efforts of partners to quit talking to each other because of the fear of more fights eventually create distance between them, both physically and emotionally. Poor communication is a vital factor that can threaten a married relationship, turning it into a toxic, unhealthy bond.

Over Possessiveness

In the initial days of married life, showing possessiveness toward your partner is a positive sign of love, care, and belongingness. Each of us feels satisfied and proud to have someone who shows their love with a gesture of possessiveness. However, a minute difference separates possessiveness as a healthy and happy exhibition of love from being trapped in the creepy shackles of obsession and insecurity. Having an overly possessive partner can be suffocating, as it can make you feel controlled, manipulated, confused, lost, and unsafe. Sometimes, failure to notice or resolve possessive behavior with your partner can make you feel stressed out, anxious, depressed, unhappy, hopeless, and have poor self-esteem, which can even lead to emotional and physical abuse.

On the other hand, being with an overly possessive partner can be detrimental not only to the married relationship but also to one's mental and physical wellness.

In severe conditions, an overly possessive partner who is unable to control their aggression can also turn violent and exhibit dangerous behaviors that could be hurtful. Factors that stir up violent acts in such scenarios are the fear of losing, a lack of trust, jealousy, and a constant need for validation and attention. When the level of over-possessiveness reaches its peak, it can cause autonomy or a lack of freedom in one's married life that leads to emotional and physical abuse, which marks the beginning of toxicity in the relationship.

Complex Financial Issues

Money can't buy happiness, yet money is a necessity for survival. Most of the time, money is regarded as the basic need that can solve most of your problems, for money answers everything. However, less known to most, money has double roles in one's life. Financial issues are an intricate and crucial topic between married couples that can initiate more minor problems in their relationship, which sometimes ends up causing toxicity. Financial matters and differences of opinion are the issues that can weaken the firm foundation of married life if they are not considered and adequately addressed. Many scenarios can become the root cause of toxicity between couples, for instance, if one partner has a lavish style of spending money, while the other has a preference to save money.

In some cases, the man is undergoing financial pressure and crisis. At the same time, the significant other is unwilling to spend her pockets to run the house, or the husband does not provide for his wife's expenditures to make her financially dependent upon him deliberately, and many more. Financial issues can impact a person's thoughts, actions, and feelings about their better half, resulting in marital dissatisfaction and hostility, ultimately eating up a marriage's charm.

Rising Ego

Often, people believe the ego to be the most sensitive element of the human psyche. It is the perception of how we look up to ourselves. When we are in a situation where we fear that our ego can be threatened or hurt in any way, we begin to exhibit defensive and aggressive behaviors. Ego is one of the root causes that can spoil married relationships. Self-centered people are mostly less likely to notice and thus overlook observing their behaviors, often because it can be too hard to handle the truth. Sometimes, most people confuse ego with self-esteem, making it an issue of pride and honor. Self-esteem is built-in confidence in oneself, while ego is a negative trait fed by positive comments and acknowledgments from external factors like other people in one's surroundings. Each of us has an ego within us, but failure to control and manage these feelings could become the reason for tremendous turmoil in your married life. Breeding ego within oneself can aggravate negative emotions like jealousy, insecurities, fear, anger, and resentment. These feelings slowly and gradually deteriorate the strong bond of love and compassion for each other, eventually turning it into a toxic relationship that is hard to strive through.

Over-Burdening Chores

As a couple grows older into their married life, their responsibilities keep increasing daily, which may sometimes be burdensome for one or both partners. It's not just the financial burden that elevates in the recent years of married life; instead, the daily household chores like managing children, cleaning the mess, preparing food for the family, and many more become the reasons that ignite an unhealthy atmosphere at home. Sometimes, when household chores are not distributed, they can become overburdening for one person, which increases the stress level tremendously. Often, factors like traditional gender roles, social policies like the unavailability of paid family leaves, and weaponized incompetence are the reasons for raising grudges and displeasing emotions between the two in a relationship. However, it is one of the essential reasons that result in an unhealthy or toxic relationship, and many times, such situations are not in one's control. Sometimes, several other elements, like sudden physical or mental illness or other familial and social pressures, make one incapable of handling such responsibilities, thereby making them unaccountable for their actions. Eventually, such an incompetent and fugitive attitude by either of the partners weakens the relationship and drags it toward a dead end.

Required Action Steps

1. Pondering over the happenings of daily life can help the couple realize and analyze the probable causes of the rising distances and differences between them.
2. After learning about the factors that trigger the onset of an unhealthy relationship, couples must look forward to sorting them out at their best.
3. While simplifying the problems between each other, the couple must be mindful of not creating new problems in their lives.

4. The couple must not make everything a reason for their clashing self-esteem, ego, and honor, as it can result in a toxic relationship.

5. Avoiding communication or running away from the problem is one of the biggest reasons that aggravates the toxicity between a couple.

When you begin to experience bumps and pitholes in the path of your relationship, then it's time to think and talk about the significant rising problems that can make your relationship a failure in the coming future. Remember to seek for help as needed. *"God is our refuge and strength, a very present help in trouble."*[2]

---

1. *Amos* 3:3
2. *Psalm* 46:1

Chapter 3

Early Warning Signs of an Unhealthy Relationship

> Who has time for toxic relationships? If someone isn't honoring your feelings, it's not a real relationship. If you feel drained after spending time with someone, that's a red flag!
>
> — Doreen Virtue, a Doctor of Psychology

Not every married relationship is the same; they vary in some aspects and keep changing with time. Having a healthy and happy relationship is often the secret shared by many successful people who believe that having the right partner choice is one of the most important decisions of one's life. The Holy Book says, "For whoever finds a wife finds a good thing and obtains favor from God." However, sometimes, knowingly or unknowingly, we may get into relationships that may harm our mental and physical health, happiness, and overall well-being. The failure to recognize the type of bond you share with your spouse is the determining factor that impacts your everyday lifestyle and future goals. In some cases, it is quite complex and problematic to identify the similar patterns that may differentiate a healthy relationship from an unhealthy one.

Signs to Look Out for in a Toxic Relationship

As most abusive and toxic relationships show clear signs and hints, some unhealthy relationships are more subtle and tricky to recognize. Apart from this, many times, a partner is aware of the toxicity in their relationship but tries to conceal and shut their eyes to the negative signs of their unhealthy relationship. In such situations, either one of the partners tries their best to make their relationship work, as they cannot face the fear of losing their loved one. However, salvaging an unhealthy and toxic relationship can deplete one's inner reserves, disconnect one from one's true self, erode one's self-esteem and self-confidence, and ultimately fragment one's well-being.

Therefore, we must acquaint ourselves with the unhealthy indicators of a relationship that incrementally steer one's marital journey toward disintegration and detachment. Recognizing these signs can serve as a life-line to prevent your fragmentation.

Misunderstandings

Having misunderstandings in a relationship is an everyday occurrence, as each partner may have varied thought processes and opinions about the same things. In a healthy relationship, usually, the couple tries to develop a mutual understanding and let go of the matter without making any big fuss about the entire scenario. However, what differentiates a healthy relationship from an unhealthy one is how the partners deal with these emerging issues. The seeds of bitterness, jealousy, competition, disrespect, incompatibility, and a lack of interest in spending quality time with your spouse are the real culprits that ignite the flames of misunder-standing to the extent that there is no turning back.

Misunderstanding is the root cause of conflicts among couples, which initiate a chain of negative emotions like stress, anxiety, frustration, and the disappointing feeling of not being understood or heard. This turmoil of depressing thoughts and emotions eventually creates distance between the couples, depleting their love, care, and empathy for each other. In the initial days of married life, when two individuals know less about each other, it is expected to have a difference of opinion that may cause misunderstanding. However, as and when the relationship progresses, each partner develops a better understanding of the other, which portrays a healthy relationship. However, in some cases, couples face extreme problems having open communication with each other, which results in constant misunderstanding and exhibits the toxicity that restricts a relationship's ability to move forward.

Frequent Quarrels

Quarrels and disagreements about a particular issue are a common sight in most marriages. But the question is, how much quarreling is enough in a normal relationship? What is the level of fighting needed to differentiate a healthy relationship from an unhealthy one? There is no single formula that can judge the type of married relationship you are in based on the number and intensity of quarrels. It is not always necessary that the reason for quarrels between the couple is a hot topic; instead, many-minute problems like mood swings, work-life pressure, and frustration with too many household chores also result in small fights among them. Having frequent fights and arguments over mundane issues causes toxicity, which eventually leads to an unhealthy relationship as it spoils the entire aura of the house.

On a different note, experts proclaim that such small quarrels don't always make a relationship bitter; instead, getting into occasional arguments can be perceived as a healthy sign. According to these studies, having fights between couples is a signal that they still care about each other, while having no arguments or conflicts is an indication that either or both partners have checked out. It is an exhibition of a lack of love and trust between couples, as they fear being judged and condemned, which restricts their ability to open up and share their true feelings.

Disrespectful Behavior

It is rightly said that marriage is a sacred relationship, but what directs happiness in married life solely depends upon the positive efforts of each partner to make it work. It's normal for every relationship to see ups and downs, while the firm foundation of trust, respect, love, and loyalty helps a relationship strive to beat all the odds of life. However, due to unfavorable or difficult situations, one may behave disrespectfully toward their partners, which initiates the never-ending cycle of hatred, disappointment, and conflicts between them. Everyone has a varied parameter for their dignity, depending on their cultural or gender connotation, and crossing that fine line and disrespecting your spouse can be shocking and hurtful. These behaviors are strong enough to leave a permanent mark and a negative impact on a person's mind that cannot be healed, even with gestures of remorse, apologies, or regret.

Sometimes, being disrespectful toward your partner is not just about being abusive verbally. At times, showing negative behaviors like dishonesty, dismissing one's needs, blocking one's communication, or comparing your partner with others also contributes to showing disrespect toward your other half. Apart from this, other signs, like being less supportive and overburdening your spouse with household chores without being helpful, can also make one feel disrespected. Many indirect ways of making one feel less in a relationship are when you do not seek their advice in critical decision-making, failing to prioritize them, mock and make fun of them, and portraying a bossy attitude. All these direct and indirect ways of giving less importance to your spouse make one feel disrespected and unvalued, which gradually creates bitterness and drift among the couple, eventually trig-gering toxicity in a relationship.

Careless Attitude

When we fall in love with someone, we embrace their habits and wear things they like just to get noticed by them. Unfortunately, sometimes, when your better half uses this as a weapon and a means to exert control over you, they show apathy and ignore such gestures, disregarding one's likes and dislikes. This careless attitude leaves them feeling unwanted and worthless. A lax attitude is an unkind expression of an absolute disregard for someone's feelings and a lack of attention to what matters to them. Ignorance can be bliss, but it can have a significant impact on the well-being of your partner, making them feel unloved, disrespected, and lonely, eventually affecting their mental and emotional health.

The most precious gift a partner can give to their spouse is their time and attention, especially if it is someone who loves you unconditionally and all they long for is your company. In a married relationship, love is nothing but caring for your significant other, doing small things that matter to them, and taking little actions that express your concern toward them. However, showing a careless attitude toward your loved ones can ruin the entire relationship and inculcate negative feelings of disappointment, disinterest, hatred, and bitterness.

Intimidation

One of the most prominent signs of a healthy relationship is that couples are not scared to approach each other, even if one is in a lousy mood, disappointed, frustrated, overburdened, or angry. Trust is the primary feeling among the partners in a healthy relationship, as it gives one confidence that they are safe and secure with them in all situations. However, sometimes, either of the partners tries to take control over the other by using negative tactics to intimidate them. Intimidation is the most common tool in the inventory of a narcissistic partner, and it is perceived as an act of using aggression, abuse, or mockery to dictate one's spouse's actions according to oneself. It is intended to disarm the intellect and decision-making ability of one's significant other and impose one's ideas and decisions on them. Partners who use intimidation tend to exploit the emotional vulnerability of their better half to exert control over them.

There could be several reasons why a partner resorts to such tactics; for example, they use them to boost their egos, feel powerful, and establish their authority over their better half. They may also use it to destroy the confidence of their spouse and make them feel worthless. Whatever the intention, ultimately, it leaves one suffering with scars that may be etched forever in their memories, eventually making one feel insecure and withdrawn from the world. Apart from this, many mental health issues can also be traced to the trauma a person has faced due to the intimidation they experienced years ago. However, by learning to stand up for oneself and knowing when to seek help, a person can save themselves from being intimidated by their partner.

Mistrust

Trust is one of the most essential pillars of a strong and healthy relationship. A relationship that lacks trust between the couples is often susceptible to negativities like increased chances of conflicts, depression, insecurity, and anxiety. Trust among partners is not developed in a single night; instead, it is a consistent effort by both to keep their promises, live up to their expectations, and be committed. However, sometimes, when either of the spouses makes it a practice and fails to align their actions with their words, it sows the seeds of mistrust between them. Gradually, consistent violations and aggressive, hurtful behavior may erode trust between the couples.

Lack of trust is one of the most common and evident signs of an unhealthy relationship. In such circumstances, it is a common view that both partners hide things from each other and are often aware of the same actions of their significant other. Talking about your daily stuff, listening, and sharing feelings are the basics that develop closeness and emotional intimacy between married couples. However, in unhealthy relationships, the spouses do not feel comfortable and at ease sharing their talks, either due to feeling judged, condemned, or fearing the onset of an argument. Often, having a past traumatic romantic experience is also one of the probable reasons for mistrust between partners, which prevents one from opening up to their current partner and initiates problems between them.

Gaslighting

Either spouse often uses gaslighting to create an environment in which their significant other starts to doubt their own beliefs. It is an artistic way that uses coercion and manipulation to alter one's perception of reality and ideology. It is also a form of emotional abuse where a partner systematically uses judgments and opinions to silence their better half and impose their narrative on them. Forcing them to adopt the new thinking that they try to impose through manipulation, consistent hostile gestures, and actions, eventually abandoning their own beliefs. The primary purpose of gaslighting one's spouse is to gain power and control over them. The impacts of gaslighting cannot be felt overnight; instead, it is a slow and gradual process that ultimately deteriorates one's self-esteem, confidence, and perception.

One of the most common ways to gaslight a partner is by lying about a real-world situation and being consistently adamant about your viewpoints to make them believe it, which creates self-doubt. At times, partners even try to gaslight their spouses by lying and denying a fact even if the other one has proof against it, which gradually changes the perception of their evidence and makes them doubt it. In some cases, either spouse tries to create a drift within your close family relations and friends by using the manipulative tactics of gaslighting merely to eliminate any chance of competition and sharing of love, which increases their partner's level of dependability upon themselves. The most common trait of a partner who uses gaslighting is that their words never match their actions. They often say one thing and do another, and living with such a personality could ultimately lead to wearing down one's partner over time. The best remedy for such a situation is to be adequately informed, enlightened, and educated to logically deduce facts, build concrete and unshakable beliefs in life, and self-reflect rather than seek validation from their partners.

Betrayal

The most fundamental component of a married relationship is trust, and betrayal is the worst thing that someone can do. A breach of trust, a broken promise, or an act of being unfaithful are all examples of betrayal. Often, partners resort to betrayal to achieve some gain; it can be power or money, but whatever the motivation behind it, it leaves your partner in a state of dismay. It can have a long-lasting impact, and a person may suffer perpetual paranoia. Betrayal does not have the exact definition for everyone, as it takes varied forms in different relationships based on the values and expectations of their partners.

An act of betrayal can take many direct and indirect forms. For instance, it can be as simple as showing highly selfish behavior or lying about something to hide the truth. At times, not supporting your partner when family and friends make fun of them or crack a joke in a public place is enough to humiliate them and give them a feeling of betrayal. In extreme situations, using the dark past of your partner against them to win an argument and make them feel smaller, or sometimes even rejecting an act of physical intimacy with your partner, can make them feel betrayed, hurt, and broken from within. Also, showing cold behavior and emotional detachment or disrespecting your partner can convey a message of betrayal, leaving one feeling lonely and emotionally withdrawn. Strong ethics, integrity, and open communication are the best ways to keep trust alive and prevent the roots of betrayal from sowing in any relationship.

Required Action Steps

1. Making a relationship better is not just knowing about your relationship and correcting its flaws; instead, it demands a good understanding of each other's behavior, likes, dislikes, and emotions.
2. Lack of trust and honesty toward your partner often becomes the critical element that triggers many differences in a relationship.
3. Look out for signs of Infidelity and betrayal from a partner by observing behavioral changes in one's partner, which may take some time.
4. Once you notice the signs of an unhealthy relationship budding between you and your partner, you must promptly communicate with

your partner peacefully and work on
improving your relationship.

5. Initiating arguments and indulging in a fight
   after exploring the truth of your relationship is
   a bad idea, and one must avoid doing so as it
   can seriously complicate the situation.

The effort for the survival of a relationship is not one-sided. It requires the cooperation, will, and dedication of both partners to make a significant change in a positive direction in their lives. Every relationship will undergo a trying time; there will be rain, wind, and flood, but having the relationship built intentionally on the rock-solid foundation of divine instructions, among other recommendations in this chapter, will keep the relation-ship standing strong.[1]

---

1. *Mathew 7:24-27*

Chapter 4

Mental Health Conditions and Unhealthy Relationships

> *Mental health problems don't define who you are. They are something you experience. You walk in the rain and you feel the rain, but you are not the rain*
>
> — *Matt Haig - British novelist*

In the complex tapestry of human relationships, hidden threads often connect mental health conditions and the quality of our partnerships. These concealed factors can silently weave toxicity and unhealthiness into the fabric of our relationships. In this chapter, we will unravel the unseen struggles, shedding light on the mental health conditions that couples may unknowingly bring into their relationships, and we will explore how to untangle these issues to build healthier and more robust connections.

Unseen Mental Health Conditions in Relationships

Many mental health conditions can go unnoticed or undiagnosed in the context of a relationship, yet they play a significant role in shaping its dynamics. Here are some of the unseen mental health conditions that can contribute to the challenges faced by couples:

Anxiety Disorders: Unseen Tormentors

Anxiety disorders are mental health situations marked by excessive and irrational fear or worry that can significantly impact an individual's life, including their relationships. These conditions often go unnoticed, yet they are among the most common mental health issues globally. Let us explore how anxiety disorders can silently torment individuals in relationships and how couples can navigate these challenges.

Types of Anxiety Disorders

- ***Generalized Anxiety Disorder (GAD)***: People with GAD experience excessive worry about various aspects of their lives, such as health, finances, work, or relationships. This persistent anxiety can make it difficult to relax and enjoy the present moment, affecting the quality of their relationships.

- ***Social Anxiety Disorder***: Social anxiety disorder manifests in a severe fear of social situations, leading to avoidance of social events or interactions; this can prevent someone from participating in their partner's social life or meeting their family and friends.

- **Panic Disorder**: Panic disorder is known for recurring and unpredictable panic attacks. These sudden episodes of intense fear can be disruptive and distressing for the person experiencing them and their partner.

- ***Obsessive-Compulsive Disorder (OCD)***: OCD involves intrusive, obsessive thoughts and compulsive behaviors or rituals. These rituals can consume time and may interfere with relationship dynamics and daily life.

- ***Post-Traumatic Stress Disorder (PTSD)***: PTSD can develop after having a traumatic event and is marked by intrusive memories, nightmares, and Hypervigilance. The emotional fallout from trauma can affect the individual's emotional availability in the relationship.

Impact on Relationships

Anxiety disorders can cast a shadow on relationships in various ways:

- *Communication Challenges*: Anxiety can make expressing one's thoughts and feelings difficult. The fear of judgment or negative reactions can hinder open and honest communication in a relationship.
- *Constant Worry*: People with anxiety disorders may worry excessively about their partner's safety, fidelity, or the relationship's future, leading to unfounded jealousy and overprotectiveness.
- *Emotional Withdrawal*: Anxiety can cause emotional withdrawal, making it challenging for individuals to provide emotional support and be present for their partner's needs.

- ***Overthinking***: Excessive rumination and overthinking can lead to misinterpretation of a partner's actions or words, causing misunderstandings and conflicts.
- ***Avoidance***: Social anxiety may lead individuals to avoid social gatherings or events with their partners, leading to isolation and frustration.

Anxiety disorders can be silent tormentors in relationships, but they need not be destructive forces. With understanding, communication, and professional help, couples can navigate the challenges posed by these conditions and build a supportive and fulfilling relationship, even in the face of anxiety.

Depression: The Weight of Unseen Darkness

Depression is an occurrence in mental health conditions that affects individuals and their relationships. It is often called the "invisible illness" because the symptoms are not always apparent, yet they can profoundly impact every aspect of a person's life, including their relationships. In this section, we will explore the complexities of depression and how it can silently affect individuals in their relationships. Depression is not merely a passing sadness or a case of the "blues." It is a clinical mental health disorder characterized by persistent and overwhelming sadness, hopelessness, and a loss of interest or pleasure in once-used activities. Critical aspects of depression include:

- **Persistent Low Mood**: Individuals with depression often experience an enduring low mood that lasts for weeks, months, or even years.

- **Loss of Interest**: They may lose interest in hobbies, work, and relationships, leading to social withdrawal and isolation.

- **Fatigue**: Physical and mental fatigue are common, making daily tasks and relationships challenging.

- **Changes in Appetite and Sleep**: Depression can disrupt eating and sleeping patterns, affecting energy levels and overall health.

- **Negative Self-Perception**: People with depression may have low self-esteem, feel guilty or worthless, and engage in self-criticism.

- **Cognitive Impairment**: Depression can

lead to difficulties with concentration, memory, and decision-making.

The Impact on Relationships

Depression is like a storm cloud that hovers over individuals, affecting their ability to engage in relationships fully. Here is how it can impact the dynamics of a relationship:

- **Emotional Withdrawal**: Depressed individuals often emotionally withdraw from their partners. They may not express affection, converse, or provide emotional support.

- **Communication Challenges**: Depression can hinder effective communication. Depressed individuals may struggle to articulate their feelings or engage in conversations about relationship issues.

- **Loss of Intimacy**: Losing interest in previously enjoyed activities can extend to intimacy, leading to a lack of sexual desire and closeness in the relationship.

- **Irritability and Conflict**: Depression can make individuals irritable and prone to conflicts, causing tension in the relationship.

- **Dependency and Codependency**: In some cases, one partner may become overly dependent on the other for emotional support, which can strain the relationship.

Depression is a weighty condition that can affect relationships, but it need not be an insurmountable challenge. With understanding, communication, and professional help, couples can navigate the complex territory of depression and build a supportive, resilient, compassionate relationship, even in the face of this invisible darkness.

Post-Traumatic Stress Disorder: The Lingering Shadow of Trauma

Trauma from past experiences can lead to PTSD, often resulting in flashbacks, emotional numbing, and Hypervigilance, making maintaining a stable and secure relationship challenging. PTSD is a complex and often debilitating mental health condition that can profoundly impact individuals, especially in the context of their relationships. It results from being involved in trauma or a series of events, and its symptoms can persist long after the traumatic experience has ended. This section will delve into the complexities of PTSD and how it can silently affect individuals in their relationships.

Understanding PTSD

PTSD can have various symptoms, often organized into four clusters:

1. ***Intrusion Symptoms***:

a. Intrusive memories, flashbacks, or nightmares result from past trauma.

b. Critical emotional distress or physical reactions when reminded of the event.

2. ***Avoidance Symptoms***:

a. Avoiding situations, people, or places that serve as reminders of trauma.

b. Persistent emotional numbing, detachment, or disinterest in activities.

3. ***Negative Alterations in Cognition and Mood***:

a. Persistent negative beliefs about oneself or others.

b. Blame, guilt, and negative emotions, such as fear, anger, or shame.

c. Decreased interest in previously enjoyed activities.

4. *Arousal and Reactivity Symptoms*:

a. Irritability, outbursts of anger, or aggressive behavior.

b. Hypervigilance, an exaggerated startle response, and not being able to concentrate fully.

c. Sleep disturbances, such as insomnia.

The Impact on Relationships

PTSD can cast a shadow over relationships in various ways:

- *Emotional Distance*: People with PTSD may emotionally withdraw from their partners, challenging providing emotional support and connection.
- *Triggers and Flashbacks*: Certain events, words, or situations can trigger flashbacks or intense emotional reactions, causing distress and confusion in the relationship.
- *Avoidance of Intimacy*: Trauma can lead to an avoidance of intimacy, making engaging in physical or emotional closeness difficult.

- ***Hyperarousal***: Symptoms like Hypervigilance and anger outbursts create tension and conflict within the relationship.
- ***Communication Challenges***: Individuals with PTSD may struggle to articulate their feelings and experiences, leading to misunderstandings and frustration.
- ***Codependency or Dependency***: In some cases, one partner may become overly dependent on the other for emotional support, which can strain the relationship.

PTSD is a profound and complex condition that can affect relationships. However, with understanding, communication, and professional help, couples can navigate the challenges posed by this condition and build a supportive, resilient, and compassionate relationship, even in the face of the lingering shadows of trauma.

Bipolar Disorder: The Rollercoaster of Emotions

Bipolar Disorder is a mental health condition noticeable by extreme mood swings, swinging between manic highs and depressive lows. This condition can significantly impact individuals' lives and relationships, creating unique challenges. In this section, we will delve into the complexities of Bipolar Disorder and how it can silently affect individuals in their relationships.

Understanding Bipolar Disorder

Bipolar Disorder involves distinct mood episodes categorized into two primary phases:

1. ***Manic Episode***:

a. During manic episodes, individuals experience an elevated, euphoric, or irritable mood.

b. Increased energy, decreased need for sleep, and heightened creativity or impulsivity may be present.

c. Risky behavior, increased talking, and difficulty focusing can occur.

2. ***Depressive Episode***:

a. Depressive episodes are characterized by prolonged periods of intense sadness, low energy, and a loss of interest or pleasure in activities.

b. Changes in appetite, sleep disturbances, guilt or worthlessness, and difficulty concentrating are common.

. . .

The Impact on Relationships

Bipolar Disorder can cast a shadow over relationships in various ways:

- **Emotional Turbulence**: The extreme mood swings can create emotional turbulence in the relationship, affecting both partners' stability.
- **Unpredictability**: The unpredictability of mood swings can be confusing and unsettling for the partner, leading to tension and uncertainty.
- **Communication Challenges**: During manic episodes, individuals may talk excessively and have racing thoughts, making it difficult for their partner to engage in meaningful conversations.
- **Risk-Taking Behaviors**: Manic episodes can lead to impulsive, risky behaviors, such as overspending, infidelity, or substance abuse, which can harm the relationship.
- **Depression-Related Withdrawal**: During depressive episodes, emotional withdrawal and low energy can lead to a lack of intimacy and support.

- ***Codependency or Dependency***: In some cases, one partner may become overly dependent on the other for emotional support, creating an unhealthy dynamic.

Bipolar Disorder is a challenging condition that can affect relationships. However, with understanding, communication, and professional help, couples can navigate the unique challenges posed by this Disorder and build a supportive, resilient, and compassionate relationship, even in the face of the emotional roller-coaster of Bipolar Disorder.

Borderline Personality Disorder (BPD): The Stormy Sea of Emotions

Borderline Personality Disorder is a complex and poorly understood mental health condition characterized by intense mood swings, unstable self-image, and impulsivity; this can lead to unpredictable behavior in a relationship and difficulties with emotional regulation. It can significantly impact an individual's life, especially in their relationships. In this section, we will explore the complexities of BPD and how it can silently affect individuals in their relationships.

Understanding   Borderline   Personality Disorder

A range of symptoms marks *BPD,* but it is primarily characterized by:

- *Intense and Unstable Relationships*: Individuals with BPD often experience intense and stormy relationships. They may idolize their partner one moment and devalue them the next.
- *Identity Disturbances*: People with BPD may struggle with self-identity, leading to emptiness and confusion about their goals, values, and relationships.
- *Impulsivity*: Impulsive behaviors are common, including reckless driving, substance abuse, binge eating, and self-harm.
- *Emotional Instability*: Intense emotional fluctuations, such as anger, sadness, or anxiety, can lead to frequent mood swings.
- *Chronic Feelings of Emptiness*: A pervasive sense of emptiness and boredom often accompanies BPD.
- *Fear of Abandonment*: Persons with BPD often have a severe fear of abandonment,

leading to clingy or reactive behaviors in their relationships.

The Impact on Relationships

BPD can create a turbulent environment in relationships in various ways:

- **Intense Conflicts**: The unstable emotional state of individuals with BPD can lead to frequent and intense conflicts in the relationship.
- **Idealization and Devaluation**: The tendency to idealize and devalue a partner can create emotional chaos and confusion.
- **Impulsive and Risky Behaviors**: Impulsivity can lead to risky behaviors that can put the relationship at risk.
- **Emotional Manipulation**: Individuals with BPD may manipulate emotionally to prevent perceived abandonment or gain attention.
- **Codependency or Dependency**: In some cases, one partner may become overly dependent on the other for emotional support, leading to an unhealthy dynamic.

- **Self-Harm and Suicidal Ideation**: In extreme emotional distress, persons with *BPD* may engage in self-harming behaviors or experience suicidal thoughts, which can be deeply distressing for both partners.

Borderline Personality Disorder is a challenging and complex condition that can affect relationships. With understanding, communication, and professional help, couples can navigate the unique challenges posed by this Disorder and build a supportive, resilient, and compassionate relationship, even in the face of the stormy sea of emotions accompanying *BPD*.

Substance Use Disorders: The Battle with Dependency

Substance Use Disorders (SUDs) are a category of mental health conditions characterized by the chronic and compulsive misuse of substances like drugs or alcohol. These disorders can have massive results on individuals' lives, especially in the context of their relationships. It can lead to deceit, broken trust, and many issues that impact the partnership's quality. In this section, we will delve into the complexities of SUDs and how they can silently affect individuals in their relationships.

Understanding Substance Use Disorders

SUDs encompass a wide range of conditions involving the misuse of substances, and they often involve:

- *Craving and Compulsion*: Individuals with SUDs experience intense cravings for the substance and have difficulty controlling their use, even when it leads to negative consequences.

- *Tolerance and Withdrawal*: Over time, the person cultivates tolerance to the substance, requiring more to achieve the desired effect. Withdrawal symptoms can occur when the substance is not used.

- *Social and Occupational Impairment*: SUDs can interfere with daily life, affecting work, relationships, and social activities.

- *Failed Attempts to Quit*: Despite multiple attempts, individuals with SUDs often struggle to quit or control their substance use.

The Impact on Relationships

SUDs can have a substantial impact on relationships in various ways:

- **Disharmony and Conflict**: Substance misuse can lead to frequent conflicts in the relationship, as the non-using partner may feel neglected or betrayed.
- **Trust Issues**: Trust is often eroded as the person with SUDs may use deceptive behavior to hide their substance use.
- **Emotional Distance**: Substance misuse can create emotional distance between partners, resulting in feelings of isolation and resentment.
- **Financial Strain**: The costs associated with substance use can place a noticeable financial burden on the relationship.
- **Codependency or Enabling**: The non-using partner may become co-dependent, enabling substance misuse, which can perpetuate the problem.
- **Safety Concerns**: Substance misuse can lead to risky behavior, putting both partners at risk and causing constant worry.

Substance Use Disorders are challenging and complex conditions that can significantly impact relationships. With understanding, communication, and professional help, couples can navigate the unique challenges posed by *SUDs* and build a supportive, resilient, and compassionate relationship, even in the face of the battle with dependency.

How unseen Mental Health Conditions impact relationships

These hidden mental health conditions can profoundly impact relationships, even if both partners are unaware of the underlying issues. Here is how they can manifest:

- ***Communication Barriers***: Anxiety, depression, and *PTSD* can hinder effective communication, resulting in misunderstandings and conflicts in the relationship.
- ***Emotional Distance***: Conditions like depression can result in emotional withdrawal, causing partners to feel isolated and disconnected.
- ***Impulsive Behaviors***: Bipolar Disorder and BPD can lead to impulsive actions,

potentially damaging trust and stability in the relationship.

- ***Insecurity and Jealousy***: Anxiety and low self-esteem can fuel insecurity and jealousy in relationships, causing unnecessary tensions.
- ***Conflict Escalation***: Unmanaged conditions can lead to heightened emotional responses during conflicts, making it challenging to resolve issues peacefully.

Required Action Steps

Recognizing the presence of these unseen mental health conditions is the first step toward healing and building healthier relationships. Here is how to begin untangling these hidden factors:

1. ***Open and Honest Communication***: This provides a safe avenue for open, non-judgmental conversations about each other's mental health and how it may affect the relationship.
2. ***Seek Professional Help***: If one suspects a mental health condition is affecting their relationship, go for help immediately. Contact a therapist or a counselor.

3. ***Educate oneself***: Learn about the specific condition and its impact on relationships. Understanding can reduce stigma and lead to more empathetic interactions.

4. ***Develop Coping Strategies***: Work together to develop coping strategies to help both partners navigate the challenges of mental health conditions.

Mental health conditions can be the unseen struggles that cast shadows over relationships. By shedding light on these hidden factors, we take the first step toward building healthier and more resilient connections. *"Keep your heart with all diligence, for out of it spring the issues of life."* [1]

---

1. *Proverbs* 4:23

Chapter 5

Codependency and Toxic Relationships

> *Addicts obsess about their "drug" of choice, whether it's alcohol, food, or sex. They plan and look forward to it. Codependents do that in relationships. Their lives revolve around someone else — especially those they love.*
>
> — *Darlene Lancer, a Renowned Author*

I n the initial days of marriage, when the couples are not engaged in fulfilling complex responsibilities of life, they share a beautiful bond by loving, caring for, and pampering each other, which makes them habitual and fond of each other. However, sometimes, getting into a married relationship with a codependent person can affect the lives and peace of mind of both partners. Sometimes, identifying and revealing that you are living in a codependent marriage can be tricky, as you feel that being addicted to one another is quite normal in a new marriage. But as time passes, the problems between the couple begin to increase if either partner is codependent. Thus, when your partner's love bothers you, it is time to explore the truth behind their behaviors. So, it is vital to explore what codependency looks like in a married relationship to help oneself cope with future issues and complications that, when not considered at the right moment, can cause toxicity in a relationship.

Understanding Codependency

Codependency is an emotional and mental barrier that impacts the way a person connects and interacts with their better half in a relationship. A codependent person over-relies on their partners, which can be considered an addiction. They need support, help, and assurance from their significant other and have an excessive psychological and emotional dependency upon them, which can be perceived as unfulfilling and toxic. A codependent partner sets high expectations from their other better half while failing to get the same love and respect from them, which could be hurtful, demeaning, depressing, and stressful, which can even initiate abusive behaviors in some situations. A codependent relationship is a demanding one that requires consistent efforts to satisfy your other half, which may sometimes lead to outbursts of emotion and loss of patience, which can be highly toxic.

Target Victims of Codependency

A codependent relationship comprises imbalanced and undivided power, wherein one person is the codependent giver, who keeps giving favors and takes care of the needs of the codependent taker. Usually, it is not easy for either of the partners to decide that they are living a codependent relationship; however, from the perspective of the third person, it becomes easy to figure out this kind of relationship between a couple. In a codependent marriage, there are equal chances that either of the partners, whether the giver or the taker, can be sought out as a victim, depending on the situation. A codependent person shows up with a combination of different features like being overly needy, addicted, immature, entitled, or troubled. These partners rely on the giver to make them feel better, compensate for their problems, and reduce the impacts of their negative behaviors. At times, the takers can be sought out as victims of the codependent relationship, as in cases when the giver is frustrated enough with doing the favors that their relationship feels burdensome. In such cases, there are chances that the giver may start misbehaving, abusing, or compromising their partner's needs for the sake of their peace and happiness.

Apart from this, a codependent giver is a person who shows traits like forgiveness, altruism, empathy, and competence and possesses an upper hand in relationships. The givers are the key supporters in taking forward a relationship, as they play the roles of rescuer, extreme caregiver, and companion. In a codependent relationship, a giver is usually the person who makes all the sacrifices and shows gestures of intense love and care by being available for their codependent partner to empower them. Thus, a codependent relationship lacks an equal share of love and care, which eventually turns into a toxic one wherein one is the victim. In most cases, a giver is often seen as the victim because they keep doing good without any expectation from their codependent partner. Sometimes, a giver may feel like they have poured enough into the relationship, which shows no signs of improving further, thus ending up in heartbreak and disappointment. Codependency can be very subtle and may be initially difficult to recognize.

Behavioral Characteristics of Codependent People

Codependency is a disturbed behavioral pattern in some people that often leads to negative feelings like anxiety, low self-esteem, and depression. Codependent partners are in constant need of support from each other as they feel the urge to be controlled by their partners or control them. Such gestures are essential for a person with this dysfunctional behavior to satisfy their emotional needs and make them feel accomplished. So, let's explore the following characteristics of a codependent partner, which can help in identifying if you are living in a codependent relationship.

1. One of the most evident traits of such partners is that they exhibit extremely controlling behavior toward their significant other.
2. Other basic signs of a codependent partner are that they fear expressing their true selves and often ignore their own needs. It is quite difficult for them to set boundaries and say no to anything that they do not want to do. Instead, they say yes to many things out of their will and happiness.

3. They are always afraid of what will happen if their partner rejects them, abandons them, or turns away toward someone else. Hence, the primary reason behind their low self-esteem and low trust in their married relationship.

4. They have strong feelings of self-doubt and inadequacy.

5. Codependent partners have the misconception that they are crucial for the survival and happiness of their significant other, which compels them to always be available for them and make sure to keep them happy no matter what.

6. The most significant need of a codependent person is to be needed by others, which makes them feel complete. When they realize that their better half can do well without their support, it arouses feelings of resentment, dissatisfaction, and displeasure.

7. These people cannot live alone and often refuse to accept help from others in their surroundings.

Drivers of Codependency

Every codependent marriage has different phases and issues; however, there are a few driving motivations that remain the same. Some similar traits that every codependent person exhibits could sometimes even become the root cause of their dysfunctional behavior. So, let's unveil the main drivers of codependency in a person, which can help one predict future problems in a married relationship and strive toward avoiding them.

1. A codependent partner is very controlling, which is driven by their insecure and fearful feeling that if they do not possess control over their better half, something unpleasant may occur.

2. The main reason that codependent partners fear saying no or setting boundaries for themselves is that they are too sensitive about hurting others, especially their significant other. The fear of losing them, hurting them, or showing selfish behavior compels them to do unwanted things.

3. A codependent person lacks self-esteem and self-confidence, which makes them feel unworthy of love. Their lives revolve around the fear of being left alone in a relationship, which could end the world for them.

4. Guilt is the biggest factor that drives codependent partners toward pleasing activities and sacrificing their happiness for the sake of their partners. They believe themselves to be accountable for others' happiness and contentment, making it a challenging task for them to change.

Codependency and Addiction

The three most important aspects of a healthy relationship are 'you,' 'me,' and 'us,' which create harmony when they are present in a balanced state. At times, when either of the three components takes up too much space in a relationship and creates an imbalance between them, it roots up the problems. Often, when the 'us' component overshadows the other two, it begins the never-ending whirl of codependency in a married relationship, which can sometimes even mask it as an addiction. There are many forms of addiction to drugs or alcohol; similarly, depending too much on your partner can make you addicted to them. When a relationship takes the form of addiction between the couple, it can drag you toward a dead-end situation where survival for your happiness and peace of mind becomes a challenging task.

Codependency and addiction are two different sides of the same coin. When you are addicted to someone due to various factors like financial dependence, love, care, or emotional connection, it becomes very challenging to behave in a stable and balanced manner. At times, fulfilling your emotional and behavioral needs can make you feel needy enough, which diminishes your ability to strive for them on your own, eventually draining you out. In such scenarios, the absence of your spouse can ultimately turn your life toward misery and pain and can sometimes even compel you to take a life-threatening action like suicide. Thus, codependency sows the seeds of extreme addiction for your significant other, which can in no time take a toxic turn not only in your married relationship but also ruin your entire life itself.

Many years back, a man died in an accident, and the wife could not be comforted. She lost all hope and wanted to die as well, and indeed, she passed within two weeks. Even though they had children, the woman felt life would be miserable without the husband and got her desire to die than to live. She left the innocent children. It was such a tragic moment - an example of codependency.

Questions to Identify Codependent Behavior

Being supportive, caring, and dependent on each other is the basis of a happy and successful marriage. While there is a fine line that differentiates a successful and healthy marriage from a codependent relationship, a codependent marriage is often one in which the powers are divided in an imbalanced manner between the couples. These relationships also have a caring, dependent, and supportive nature toward each other. Still, it is just a little more than usual, which eventually becomes a demanding task that drains out the energy, positivity, and enthusiasm from within a partner or both couples. So, it is imperative to identify a codependent marriage before it is too late to take up the charge and wipe off the ingrained issues between the couples. In this context, the below questions could make it easy for one to understand and become aware of codependent behaviors.

1. Does the happiness, emotions, behaviors, and expectations of your partner become a liability, a responsibility, or the most important priority of your life?

2. Does spending time on yourself for self-care make you feel guilty for not being with your partner?

3. Does being alone for a while, without your spouse, bother you, arouse negative thoughts of being left alone, or make you anxious?

4. Does spending time alone affect your peace and calmness, making you feel restless?

5. Does speaking out for yourself, making a small request, or having open communication with your partner seem like a demanding task to you, which can aggravate tension and arguments between the two of you?

6. Does setting healthy boundaries within your relationship create new problems for you and your better half, eventually complicating the situation?

Fixing Codependent Relationships

Often, one fails to realize at an early stage that a code-pendent relationship gradually traverses toward a toxic one, which ultimately could have a sad and painful ending. Like every relationship, even this one begins with immense love, care, and respect for each other. However, the codependent behavior of either or both partners slowly begins to weaken the foundation of the marriage bond, which becomes a burden for both. Thus, even against your desires, will, and comfort, either partner would seek a permanent separation as the best way to deal with the exhausting and frustrating situation. At the same time, if a person realizes what harm their codependent attitude can do to their relationship, they will make an effort at the earliest to change their behavior to avoid a hurtful situation. Therefore, let's discover the simple tricks to help soothe our curious minds by finding the best solution to save a codependent relationship from becoming toxic.

1. Whenever you think of approaching your partner, be mindful and never forget to question your intentions. Practicing mindfulness in a married relationship can help avoid any act ending in codependency.

2. Always self-analyze how you feel and behave with your significant other. Being conscious of your feelings can avoid any complications in the relationship without creating a burden for each other.

3. Whenever you feel doubtful that you are living in a codependent marriage, you better spare some precious time and sit alone to

contemplate how you can improve the situation.

4. Get out of your comfort zone and do things you fear.

5. Never hesitate to make your own decision. Being accountable for your life and choices can make you feel confident and save you from regretting who you are and what you achieve.

6. Never be too judgmental about each other. Share a space where both can confront each other and feel optimistic about such gestures.

7. Setting healthy boundaries is the basis for having a happy, healthy, and harmonious married life.

8. Taking a break in your married life is a good practice that helps boost confidence and trust and teaches you to be honest with your significant other. Spending time away from each other sometimes, for a few days, can also help reignite the love between the couples.

9. Be responsible for your happiness and save your partner and the relationship by trying to help you find your peace and joy. Remember, a positive and happy person has the right vibes to spread positivity and happiness around themselves too.

10. Learn to have an optimistic outlook on criticism in marriage without taking it too personally or being offended.

11. Spend some time focusing on yourself. A negligent person who hardly bothers about their happiness can do no good and make no effort to make their spouse happy.

12. Make it a habit to invest time in something that you like and that can help you build your identity. Remember that there exists life beyond marriage, too.

13. Accept yourself just the way you are. Never try to change yourself to please your soulmate, as this ends true love and starts an exhausting journey of conditional love.

Required Action Steps

1. Depending on one's partner for a few things is completely fine, as marriage is a mutual relationship, and it is impossible for one to exist and flourish independently.

2. Taking your partner's help and providing them with your support is a good gesture that can strengthen the relationship. However, being

excessively dependent on your partner for everything can make you handicapped and irresponsible.

3. It is often difficult for couples to figure out the existence of codependency in their relationship, as it is misinterpreted as usual helping behavior, so one should be mindful to prevent becoming addicted to one's partner.

4. Practice self-reflection to understand your behavior, which can help you determine if you are on the path of codependency.

5. Observe your partner for any signs of codependency and try to help them cordially to prevent your relationship from drowning in the swamp.

To live an everyday, happy life, one must always try to maintain everything within a given limit, as an excess of anything, whether love or codependency, can cause toxicity in a relationship. *"Have you found honey? Eat only as much as you need, lest you be filled with it and vomit"* [1]

---

1. *Proverbs 25:16*

Chapter 6

Impact of an Unhealthy Relationship

> A bad relationship can do that, can make you doubt everything good you ever felt about yourself.
>
> — *Dionne Warwick, an American Singer*

Getting hurt, betrayed, or being a victim of an unhealthy relationship can be extremely overwhelming, which leaves a dark impression on one's mind, impacting not only the present but also putting the entire future at stake. As every person is different, they exhibit dissimilar coping abilities and skills for taking up the challenges of dealing with these demeaning moments and memories, which can have a severe long-term impact. Living in a dysfunctional relationship can not only erode one's sense of self-worth and self-esteem but could also change one's entire perception of oneself. Each day, looking at oneself in the mirror gives one a sinking feeling that the only identity one is left with is the one given to one by one's toxic partner. Even after getting separated from them and coming out of an exhausting relationship, sometimes some people may not be able to get over their past completely; instead, they begin to imagine themselves through the eyes of their toxic spouses. The damage is so harsh and intense that it cannot be healed even with the help of yearlong therapies and counseling. At times, the ever-lasting impacts of an unhealthy relationship can also bother a person in the form of various personality disorders. So, let us explore some of the severe visible implications of an unhealthy relationship, which are strong enough to flip one's life upside down if not taken care of at the right time.

Visible Changes Due to a Toxic Relationship

Living in an unhealthy relationship can not only create troubles in one's married life, but it can also have extreme negative impacts that are visible in other parts of one's life as well. Being in a toxic relationship can affect one both mentally and physically, and it distracts one from concentrating on other important aspects of life. So, it is crucial to have an idea about the significant, long-term, and sometimes lasting impacts of an unhealthy and toxic relationship to save oneself from bearing any extreme and permanent losses.

Disturbs Mental Health

As man is a social animal, our brains are programmed to live in harmonious and social relationships with other people that can help in sharing and expanding our intellect and building our personalities. However, when one starts living in a relationship that becomes burdensome, unhealthy, and toxic, it can result in a greater level of stress, anxiety, and depression in one's life. Living in such conditions for extended periods can trigger the stress response system in our body, which releases higher levels of cortisol, the stress-relieving hormone. In contrast, extreme exposure to a higher cortisol level can gradually impact mental balance and soundness.

The harmful and displeasing behaviors in a toxic relationship are responsible for creating an emotional imbalance and distress within a person, such as belittling, criticism, manipulation, control, abuse, and violence, which gradually take the form of low self-esteem, stress, and anxiety. Sometimes, being consistently controlled and condemned by one's partner also initiates negative feelings of fear and doubt in one's mind, eventually deteriorating their self-confidence and their ability to face other people. These behavioral changes due to extreme mental impact may create distance between one and other vital relationships in life, like family and friends. At times, it also interferes with one's regular sleeping pattern due to recurring depression, which drags one toward isolation.

Disrupts Career

Aspiring for successful career opportunities has always been one of the most blamed issues, which leads to poor understanding and conflicts in a married relationship. It is believed that being more involved in one's professional life often complicates issues on the personal front. Thus, due to mismanaged work-life balance and mismatched opportunities, couples can hardly dream of a happy married life. However, often the reverse of this scenario also occurs. Research has revealed that having a happy but intimate, stable, and quality marriage is essential to success in one's professional life (Aries, 2016). This research claims that a happy and healthy person is likelier to have a focused, productive, and creative bottom line.

Many times, in the rush to achieve our professional goals, we forget that the road that takes us toward success comprises basic familial support, including one's spouse, who comforts one with praises, hopes, compliments, and unconditional love. Being in a toxic relationship could not only distract one from concentrating but also weaken one emotionally and mentally, draining away one's capabilities to perform at one's best and thereby disrupting one's career drastically.

Degrades Physical Health

Most of us often misinterpret that a toxic relationship can influence our emotional and psychological well-being alone. However, research has claimed that unhealthy relationships work more like a silent killer that gradually weakens us and thus deteriorates our physical health too. Such draining relationships are more like energy vampires who keep sucking good health and happiness from one's life. For instance, living in a constant state of stress can have a direct impact on one's heart health. Based on research, people living in toxic relationships have an increased probability of 34% of heart-related problems compared to those who live in happy families (Khan, 2018). Compared to normal and healthy relationships, around two-thirds of people in unhealthy married relationships have a reduced life span of about 11 years (Khan, 2018). Apart from this, being consistently in stressful and negative situations also impacts the ability of one's body to fight against various illnesses and diseases, ultimately affecting the immune system. Further, higher stress is directly involved in changing one's healthy eating habits into binge eating and thus promoting a sedentary lifestyle, which automatically pushes people toward an unhealthy lifestyle, causing obesity and other chronic issues.

Dooms Relationships

The invasion of toxicity in a relationship not only creates issues that affect one's mental and physical health but can also have adverse effects spread beyond one's expectations. In some cases, where the level of misunderstandings, arguments, and conflicts crosses the limit, the couples begin to lose hope in each other, which results in no more fights or silence between them. However, silence can help sort out the conflicts between the two, but it is not always a good sign. In such unhealthy relationships, where there is no scope for love and affection left between the couples, lack of communication is just another form of exhibiting one another's disinterest in carrying the relationship forward. As these couples believe that there is nothing much to discuss or argue about, they end up embracing silence and cutting off from each other, which often marks the death of a relationship. Apart from all this, the bitterness and differences that develop due to these daily rising conflicts, abuse, and violence leave no room for any compromise or restart of the relationship.

Required Action Steps

1. Dwelling on the misfortunes of the past only worsens the situation and impacts one's overall lifestyle; thus, it is advisable to involve oneself in things that could help one get over the hurtful memories.

2. Seek help from a therapist or a medical practitioner at an early stage to reduce the harsh and severe mental and emotional impacts of living in a toxic relationship.

3. When one feels overstressed and anxious, it is better to talk to a close friend, family member, or spiritual counselor about one's concerns, which could help relieve the tension and improve one's ability to concentrate on one's professional goals.

4. One should engage in new activities and hobbies to divert one's mind from depressing thoughts, which could help boost mood and confidence.

5. One should focus more on reducing one's mental stress and emotional trauma, as these are the key reasons that impact one's physical health and career goals and cause irritability and a lack of concentration.

It is very challenging for one to live in a toxic relationship as it can create miseries in one's life; however, taking the proper steps to avoid these harsh impacts can help improve the situation to a great extent. *"Where there is no counsel, the people fall; But in the multitude of counselors there is safety."* [1]

---

1. *Proverbs 11:14*

Chapter 7

Tips to Heal a Broken Relationship

> If *you walked away from a toxic, negative, abusive, one-sided, dead-end, low vibrational, relationship or friendship – you won.*
>
> — Lalah Delia, a Spiritual Writer

A s we live in this world and engage ourselves in various chores, we often get hurt. It does cause us pain, but still, we continue the journey of our lives with the hope that every wound will heal and all the pain will subside. Likewise, while living in a relationship close to our hearts and contributing to various special memories, we sometimes fail to maintain its charm and love. This may bring our relationship to a turning point where everything looks devastated, and the journey toward mending the broken relationship seems like a big task. Experts reveal that only 60% of couples enjoy the pleasure of living a happy life after marriage, and the rest of the 40% of marriages end up as disasters (Basile, 2016). However, with some specific steps in the right direction, a positive attitude, and faith in God, one can surely improve their relationship and life. So, let's master the art of healing and mending one's love life by working on the vital aspects of building a relationship.

Setting Healthy Boundaries

In our lives, we are blessed with numerous relationships, and each relationship has its own limits and boundaries. The term boundaries are often misinterpreted as a big hindrance that comes in the way of the flourishing of a good and healthy relationship. But the truth is contrary, as boundaries are not always bad. Setting healthy boundaries is the first thing that a married couple must think about and work on once they enter a relationship to maintain its charm and happiness. It is one of the vital factors that helps an individual balance the yin and yang of a married relationship. Boundaries can be anything that defines a restricted fine line between you and your partner, helping one maintain their self-respect, dignity, and importance.

Need for Healthy Boundaries

Like every other important thing required to help your relationship bloom, setting healthy boundaries between you and your partner is also the need of the hour, which assists in maintaining attraction and love in your married life. There are many justified reasons for which one must set these boundaries in a relationship. So, let's dig deeper to explore and understand the need to work on setting healthy boundaries in a relationship.

1. It can help nourish your relationship by teaching respect and love for each other.
2. It can combat the negativity in your relationship by sorting out misunderstandings and doubts.
3. It can boost your and your partner's self-esteem by defining the limits of a relationship.
4. It can improve the overall quality of a relationship by reducing stress, anxiety, and confusion.

Tips to Set Healthy Limits and Boundaries

At times in life, when you don't set certain limits between yourself and your partner, things seem to go out of your control, which may make you feel frustrated and become a reason for increasing distance between the two. The rules and limits in a marital relationship are not like those in a school or some professional firms, where the authority presents a defined set of rules, and all are bound to abide by them. Instead, a healthy and happy marriage requires boundaries that are set mutually with the consent and will of both partners, thereby giving a new definition and outlook to the relationship. So, let's get going with some vital tips to stay longer in a healthy relationship with your partner by defining your boundaries.

1. Give yourself some time to know and understand what you want from your relationship and your partner by reflecting on your cultural background, values, thoughts, and beliefs. One of the simplest ways to do so is to self-interrogate by asking yourself various questions.
2. It would help if you thought deeply about how your partner and the relationship you are

living in makes you feel. This can help you analyze your true feelings and emotions toward your partner and help you define the correct boundaries for a healthy relationship.

3. Discuss your needs and expectations about the relationship with your partner openly. This can be achieved by having clear and fearless conversations, which may help you relate to and respect each other's boundaries and limits.

4. You ought to entertain your partner's queries and doubts regarding anything you set as boundaries with patience. It is a necessary step, as it may provide more clarity and better understanding to your partner by helping them follow the boundaries in a committed manner.

5. It would help if you made it a duty to implement the boundaries you have set in your relationship in a very discreet way.

6. You must listen to, accept, and respect the boundaries set by your spouse, too. This interactive gesture marks the commencement of a positive, friendly, and healthy relationship in one's life.

Dos and Don'ts While Setting Healthy Boundaries

While defining boundaries in a relationship, one must avoid crossing the limits and making one's partner feel like a prisoner. Often, when creating a healthy relationship, we end up making a mess out of the situation, which can eventually result in toxicity between the couple. Thus, it is essential to have a comprehensive understanding of the necessary things that must be done to improve the quality of one's life. So, below are a few interesting ways to mark the beginning of a fruitful marriage by setting acceptable boundaries for your relationship.

1. Remember to pay attention to the boundaries set by others, as this may make them uneasy and annoyed.
2. Do give sufficient space and freedom to your partner in a relationship, as it may let your relationship grow and blossom.
3. Don't adopt codependent behaviors in your relationship, as this may overburden your partner.

4. Treat your partner with equality and compassion, as this will make your relationship respectable.

5. Don't show your monopoly as a stronger one in a relationship, as this may create complex ego issues.

6. Do exhibit flexible and understanding behavior toward your partner, which may lead to healthy communication.

7. Don't ask irrelevant grilling questions from your spouse, as this may show your mistrust and doubtful attitude.

8. Do display a sense of responsibility in a relationship, which may make you feel more empowered.

9. Don't indulge in unnecessary arguments and conflict, which may be emotionally draining.

Fight, But Make Peace Later

Having fights and minor arguments in a married relationship is expected, but when followed by misunderstandings and days of silence, it may give a bitter turn to a relationship. However, silence is the best tool to finish off an argument and aim for peace, but when someone confines themselves after a fight, it becomes an unhealthy gesture, which results in building up negativity in the minds of both people in a relationship. One must give sufficient space and freedom of speech to one's partner in a relationship by letting them express themselves without the fear of being judged and criticized. This reduces the scope of persistent fights, converting them into productive arguments. Thus, respecting each other's thoughts, valuing their opinions, and sorting out any minor disputes or heated debates will help one develop a friendly and healthy relationship in life. So, let's endeavor to comprehend the possibility of conflicts and fights in our lives by undermining the reasons that lead to these traumatic events.

Reasons for Conflicts Between a Couple

It is a must to know the probable causes that often create unmanageable conflicts to sort out the differences between each other in a marriage, which tend to toxify the relationship. A conflict can be understood as any disagreement in thoughts and ideas or misunderstood conversations that may create major differences between a couple. It can be over any hot topic of the day: mismanaged financial burdens, unshared house-hold responsibilities, unsatisfied relationship goals, etc. Dealing with this requires a proper vision and a broader perspective to understand your spouse better. So, let's explore the common root causes that trigger these frequently rising issues and make our lives a big challenge.

1. When either of the partners tries to take control in a relationship by exhibiting dominant behavior and power, thereby making the other one feel inferior.

2. When one of the partners behaves selfishly without considering the needs and desires of the other, it induces an offensive feeling in the heart of the suffering partner, thereby drifting the two apart.

3. When your relationship becomes prey to over-criticism at the hands of either partner, the fear of being judged often hinders the relationship from blooming and flourishing into a healthy one.

4. When the fear of being misinterpreted and ignored overpowers the process of healthy communication between a couple, the relationship may be in danger of becoming intoxicated.

5. When the level of expectations set by either of the partners is too high, or if one of the partners fails to come up to the mark in terms

of meeting the other's expectations, the
relationship may turn bitter in no time.

6. When there are any unmet desires of either of
   the partners in terms of financial stability,
   emotional support, physical intimacy, or social
   status, it may cause grudges and eventually
   affect the relationship.

Essential Steps to Resolve the Conflicts in a Marriage

Exhibiting defensive behavior and overpowering one's partner may often occur when we try to win an argument and prove ourselves right in a relationship. However, such aggressive behavior can be detrimental to the survival of both individuals involved in a relationship. When a heated argument takes the form of a severe fight, then one never fails to point fingers at the other, thereby condemning, raising voice, and defaming the opponent partner, which eventually hurts the emotions and sentiments and aggravates the issue that becomes more difficult to resolve. So, instead of making your day-to-day problems a cumbersome issue, one should adopt these few easy-peasy steps to resolve the conflicts without creating much fuss about them.

1. Investigate the core issues in your life that often become the reason for conflicts and arguments in your relationship.
2. Focus on one major issue at a time to get better results and prevent overburdening both partners.
3. Find a feasible solution to the issue, considering the sensitive aspects of your relationship.
4. Discuss all the possibilities with your partner and decide on the best solution to the problem to move forward mutually.
5. Cordially implement agreeable measures to sort out the issue in the most efficient manner.
6. Create room for welcoming any new changes in the plans to help you and your partner cope with resolving the conflicts.
7. Work out each disputed issue in your relationship similarly to feel the difference in the long run.
8. Look for any improvements in your relationship after including these simple steps.

Rekindling the Passion

In the long run, constant conflicts and misunderstandings often make things very different for the couple. In such situations, it becomes difficult to communicate the hope and desire to rekindle the love and passion in the marital relationship. In most cases, there are hardly any chances of remaking the chemistry between the two as the couple begins to ignore each other, thereby avoiding any scope for communication and sharing space, leading to a breakdown in the relationship.

Tips to Improve Intimacy

Many times, the efforts to reconnect with your partner may make you feel awkward and giddy, but you never know if this new start can take you toward exploring new heights of love, passion, and intimacy between you and your partner. So, let's dig out the possibility of reigniting the spark of your love life again by creating a romantic aura.

1. Spare time to sit together and talk about the good old days, reminiscing about the beautiful memories you both cherished and nurtured before your relationship drifted apart.

2. Try to sort out all the misunderstandings by indulging in fruitful conversations with each other and becoming active listeners to your partner.

3. Take initiative in making love with your partner and never deny it when your partner approaches you to share an intimate moment.

4. Always compliment your partner for everything, no matter how minor, to make them feel special and wanted, as it will attract them toward you and trigger the hidden emotions of love and closeness.

5. Practice exhibiting physical gestures like cuddling, kissing, touching, and passing smiles, as it will give your partner indications that you are ready to rekindle the passion between each other.

If Nothing Works, Think About Your Relationship Again

Many times, it happens that despite putting in lots of effort and working on a relationship, we never see any progress or chance to save it from reaching its ultimate end, which can be disheartening on the part of a dedicated partner. In such a situation, it is customary to become confused, worried, and guilty about the negativities surrounding one completely. However, to cope with it, one needs to spare some time to sit in peace, think over their relationship once again, and look out for various signs and indicators that can help one decide whether their relationship can be saved or whether it has no scope for a restart.

Signs a Marriage Is ill-fated

Living under the same roof and after sharing years of togetherness, it is a challenging task to end the relationship. And when it is about unconditional love, young kids, and financial insecurity, one must think twice before embracing the decision to back off from a relationship. At the last minute, one expects things to get sorted out between the two so that everything can get back on track. But sometimes, it is not, and one cannot deny them. So, instead of hurting yourself, look out for any of these unpleasant pointers that can mark the roadblock in marriage.

1. One of the worst and most hurtful acts a partner begins to exhibit is stonewalling. In such a situation, the partner stops any discussion or argument in the middle of the conversation and leaves no scope for the other

person to express or convey their point of view. Thus, this act shuts all the doors to communicating with each other, showing complete detachment from the partner.

2. At times, the toxicity in the relationship surpasses all limits. It compels either of the partners to create distance from the other by opting for physical separation. In such a case, the two partners don't share any space together and begin to live in different rooms and dine alone. Thus, it initiates the process of distancing from one another, which is one of the most prominent signs that the relationship is chronic.

3. In a drowning marital relationship, it is typical to have differences of opinion, which may also result in arguments and criticism. But when these take the form of verbal abuse and physical violence, then take it as a warning sign that the relationship is not working anymore and may end up hurting either of the two if appropriate care is not taken on time.

4. Many of the reasons mentioned above often become the trigger, pushing your partner away from you.

Signs a Marriage Can Flourish

Marriage is a lifelong commitment that endures until one of the partners passes away. In the same vein, some continue to cherish their relationships even after losing their partners, demonstrating the enduring strength of marriage to unite two distinct individuals into one harmonious union. There are moments when life's challenges lead us to entertain negative thoughts and impulsively consider drastic changes. Yet, before making any decision that could dramatically alter our lives, it is imperative to reflect on the facts and discerning signs that may guide us toward preserving our relationships. Therefore, here are several crucial qualities to look for in your partner's behavior, which can offer a glimmer of hope for the revival of your marital bond amid the darkness of a toxic and unhealthy relationship.

1. Regardless of your problems in your married life, if your partner accompanies you to some family function, a doctor's place, or your child's parent-teacher meeting, you must take it as a sign that your partner still cares for you and your well-being.

2. Arguments don't always mean that a person is unwilling to listen to you or is not accepting

your thoughts and ideas; instead, some disputes initiated by your partner may aim to make you understand their perspective and can be an attempt to save the ill-fated marriage. So, if your partner argues with you and tries to communicate, give them your ears and save your marriage.

3. In extreme fights, if there are instances of any verbal abuse or physical violence between the two of you, your partner immediately feels guilty about it and apologizes to you. Then, you must exhibit your compassion and generosity by forgiving your partner and giving them another chance in your married life.

4. If your partner still loves to have a glimpse of you, compliments you, or tries to build physical intimacy with you, that shows that your partner continues to be emotionally attached to you and is reluctant to deny your existence. So, take advantage of this golden opportunity to give your relationship a new start by embracing the good and the bad in your partner and reliving your married life.

Required Action Steps

1. Sit with your partner in a calm and relaxing place to talk peacefully about your priorities and expectations of each other.
2. Plan a short vacation with your spouse to reignite the spark of love and intimacy between you.
3. Practice compassion and kindness to make them feel loved and pampered.
4. Try to give up on arguments, as quitting doesn't always mean you are weak; sometimes, it means you are strong enough to let go.
5. Step into your partner's shoes to understand what they are going through and determine their perception.

As they say, breaking a relationship is easy, but making one is too hard, as it may take a lifetime. Thus, be empathetic - be mindful of your words, actions, and decisions. *"Place me like a seal on your arm; for love is as strong as death."* [1]

MAKE A DIFFERENCE WITH YOUR REVIEW

Unlock the Power of Generosity

> Kindness is like a boomerang. It always comes back.

Hey Awesome Reader,

Just like you, I believe in the power of making a difference. Imagine helping someone you've never met, someone seeking guidance in the maze of relationships. That's where you come in.

Would you take a moment to help a someone by leaving a review for Freedom From Unhealthy Relationships? It's a simple act that takes less than 60 seconds but can change someone's life forever. Here's why your review matters:

- Your words might guide one more couple towards healthier, happier relationships
- Your insights could support someone in navigating the complexities of marriage
- Your review might be the encouragement someone needs to break free from toxicity

To leave your review, visit https://www.amazon.com/review/review-your-purchases/?asin=1962758001   or Scan the QR Code

SCAN TO REVIEW

I can't wait to share more valuable insights with you in the upcoming chapters. Thank you from the depths of my heart.

Yours truly,

Joseph Ajayi.

PS - Here's a cool fact: Your Kindness not only helps others but also makes you more valuable to them. If you know another couple or single who could benefit from this book, share the love and send it their way.

---

1. SOS 8:6

Chapter 8

Giving up on a Toxic Relationship

> It is better for someone to break your heart once by leaving your life, than for them to stay in your life and break your heart continually.

— *Terry Mark, a Renowned Writer*

Often, sitting alone and contemplating ourselves, we imagine our lives to be filled with immense happiness and tranquility with people whom we love. These people form our natural support system, morning sunshine, and the secret to feeling reenergized in this competitive world. However, reality is far beyond one's imaginary world of perfection, as most of the time, the person we fall in love with is the same one who hurts us the most. The need to be loved unconditionally by our soulmates sometimes costs more than our expectations.

Sometimes, when you realize that your married relationship no longer has that charm but is instead filled with loveless, stingy, hostile, and bitter memories, and having done all that is required to make it work and the challenges persist, it probably might be the time to move on and refresh these pages of life. Thinking about parting with your loved one may sound easy and simple, but it can prove to be the hardest thing to implement. Please understand that simply opting for a divorce is not the solution to an unhealthy married relationship, as the glimpse of the dark shades of your married life keeps haunting you in the form of flashbacks, stealing away your peace of mind. So, count the cost before deciding to let go of your marriage. However, letting go of a toxic relationship will help to enhance the following:

Improving One's Mental and Physical Health

An unhappy and toxic married life can dramatically impact one's mental and physical health. In an unhealthy relationship, an individual is always surrounded by different types of fears, like fear of being hurt, fear of being disowned, fear of being socially embarrassed, etc. However fear is a physical gesture, but it triggers the release of hormones like cortisol and adrenaline in our body, which results in increased stress and anxiety. In a stressful situation, the body's blood pressure and heart rate also fluctuate, which increases the tendency of heart attacks, strokes, and various other chronic illnesses in an individual. Apart from this, constant physical abuse from the partner can make one weak and afflicted, thereby making one's life a painful and traumatic journey. In the worst scenario, these mental and physical traumas can lead to death, either by murdering their torturous spouse or by indulging in self-harming acts like suicide.

Raising Happy Children

Couples often fail to realize that constant fights and quarrels are the foremost reasons that can impact the minds and thoughts of their young, growing children. Looking at the imperfect and toxic relationship between one's parents can leave a dark and negative impression on the child's mind regarding marriage and life after. Children learn from the live examples and actions of their parents. Thus, portraying an unhealthy relationship could scare the child from getting into such bonds once they grow up and teach them the immoral way of reacting and behaving in a given situation. It's important to teach a child that a successful marriage is the result of consistent efforts, compromise, respect, love, and sacrifices for each other. However, when a marriage attracts negativity and toxicity, that is when the idea of separation or divorce sets in, contrary to the original plan of marital bliss.

Redefining One's Better Self

No individual can be regarded as toxic or depressed in a marriage unless one exhibits signs of some mental or behavioral disorder. Living in an unwanted relationship compels one to forcefully fulfill one's duties and various actions in life, which makes one feel frustrated and irritated. In such situations, it is evident for an individual to exhibit negative emotions along with unfriendly behavior, which is not the reality of that individual. Thus, concerns and the negative happenings of life play a significant role in making one a manipulative and controlling freak. At times, putting in efforts to reverse an unhealthy marriage is enough to cause an emotional breakdown, which may compel them to behave wrongly.

Signs of distress in a marital relationship

Marriage is a happy place, but it is not the same for many. Life bestows challenges on everyone in different phases and diverse ways. Sometimes, these come in the form of an unhealthy marital relationship, which has the power to drastically impact your entire life, perspective, and future. Opting for divorce is not always the right option; perhaps it is an inappropriate choice, but at times, if it can heal your wounds or save your life, it is something that can be considered. Based on research, divorce is quite common in the United States, with at least half of marriages ending in permanent separation. Based on this analysis, it is found that at least 40 to 50 percent of first marriages end in divorce, while around 60 to 65 percent of second marriages opt for a permanent separation in the United States (Kenneth, 2020). Thus, it becomes necessary to understand the pit holes in a relationship that push one toward the decision of divorce.

Even if you have been married for more than a decade or just a few months, opting for divorce is a challenging task. Taking this harsh step can take a toll on your entire thought process as the world seems to diminish before your eyes. However, as every being is unique, so are their married lives and challenges, which cannot be compared or judged in any way by anyone. Here is a list of a few signs that show distress in a marital relationship

1. When there is no scope for fruitful and happy communication in your married life. Both partners exhibit unwillingness and hesitation to initiate any further communication with each other because of the fear of fights, disappointments, and abuse.

2. When your married relationship does not have intimacy. The feeling of closeness or intimacy is the basis that brings two people close enough to increase their fondness for each other. Many reasons result in a lack of intimacy between partners, like infidelity, being hurt, hatred, and bitterness in one's mind.

3. When either of the partners tries to create financial hardship or isolation for the other, it marks the end of love, compassion, kindness, and concern for each other.

4. When investing in a married relationship is not a top priority anymore. Such condemning behavior portrays a gesture lacking respect, consideration, and interest in nourishing one's relationships.

5. When the level of toxicity surpasses all limits. This is depicted by the onset of abuse, violence, and a lack of respect, love, and mutual understanding between spouses.

6. After counseling, therapy, and spiritual guidance, both parties are still adamant about change and willing to cooperate.

Things That Make Giving Up Difficult

Ending a marital relationship is a profoundly challenging endeavor. For many individuals, even contemplating the prospect of separating from their once-beloved partner, with whom they once envisioned a blissful life, can elicit intense emotions and physical reactions. While there is a possibility that a relationship can improve and one can once again find happiness with one's soulmate, the decision to remain in or leave a relationship is deeply influenced by one's personal experiences, beliefs, life stories, expectations, and resilience. What may seem relatively straightforward for one person could be an agonizing journey over hot coals for another. Therefore, it's crucial to delve into and comprehend the diverse reasons that continually sway an individual's mind each time they contemplate ending a toxic relationship and embarking on a path toward a life filled with peace and happiness. Here are some of them:

* * *

Fear of an Uncertain Future

The decision to part with your soulmate is a daunting one that takes a toll on your emotions and your courage. At times, in the heat of the moment, one may decide that divorce is the best solution for getting rid of a depressing relationship. However, at other times, millions of weird thoughts may occupy your mind and make you feel uncertain about taking this big decision in life. The toxicity of the current relationship inculcates such fear and doubt within one's mind that you begin to feel lost and confused. Questions like 'What would happen to my kids?', 'Will I ever find someone who loves me unconditionally?', 'Does this relationship still have a chance to get better?' or 'How will I survive alone forever?' keep haunting you like an absolute nightmare. Thus, our mind keeps hovering over the various positive and negative aspects and options that life would imply for us.

Guilt of Breaking a Relationship

One of the prominent signs that differentiate a healthy relationship from an unhealthy one is the consistent thoughts of guilt, shame, blind loyalty, and detrimental obligations. While in a toxic relationship, leaving your partner to fill their mind with concerning thoughts like it may ruin their life or make them feel all alone, you begin to blame yourself for making their life miserable and ruining their future. Thus, negative emotions like guilt are rooted within your mind and consistently stop you from thinking about your happiness and peace.

Lack of Self-Confidence

Many times, a person lacks the required self-confidence to take any extreme step that could completely break their married relationship. For some people, permanent separation is like a big failure in life. It is more like a prestige issue or a label to satisfy their egos. In such a situation, they lack the motivation to get away from an unhealthy relationship, as it could make them feel like a loser and make them hopeless about their future life. Thus, the consistent thoughts of divorce are muddled up in a person's mind, making them more confused, anxious, and worried about their life and happiness.

Emotional Bond With the Partner

Marriage is a special bond that begins with love, care, and a shared promise between the couples that no matter what happens, they will stand by each other's sides. In some cases, these feelings of love and the shared bonds are so impactful and ingrained within a person's mind that they keep questioning themselves about hurting the one they love the most. It is challenging for a person like this to gather the courage to opt for a divorce, even in the face of apparent toxicity, as it marks the end of the shared emotional bond with their partner.

Concern About Children

No doubt, divorce is not a praiseworthy option, as it not only ends the relationship between two mature people but could also harm the young, innocent, and immature minds of your children. The happenings and the bad experiences during one's childhood have a solid and long-lasting impact on a kid's mind that keeps haunting them even as they grow up into mature adults. Sometimes bitter childhood experiences like witnessing the cries and hues of their parents' divorce can cause persistent anxiety, stress, irritability, or intense sadness within them, which causes depression. However, at times, the impacts can be strongly deteriorating for them, as it causes extreme behavioral problems and creates trouble forming any new relationships when they grow up. Thus, being aware and thoughtful about these consequences could prevent a person from breaking up an unhealthy relationship.

* * *

Manipulative Tactics of the Toxic Partner

In some relationships, either partner uses manipulative tricks and tactics to control the other. They use control techniques to create a strong sense of dependency on their partner and on themselves, which slowly diminishes their self-confidence to survive alone. In some cases, these manipulating partners also identify the insecurities of their partner and try to intensify them to make them feel more clueless. At times, these manipulative partners also trick you by showing immense love or intense affection towards you to keep you wandering and puzzled about the entire situation. Thus, in such circumstances, it becomes difficult for one to analyze if one must opt for taking an extreme step or not.

Social and Religious pressure

In some cases, when a person comes from a family background and a religious belief where extreme actions like divorce are considered a social taboo and looked down upon, it becomes difficult for them to make this decision. In such scenarios, a person is stuck in a fight within themselves, as their morals and values preach that it is wrong to opt for separation while their mind and heart are suffering, instead impacting their peace of mind and physical health. Further, at times, living and being brought up in a family and religion where bearing abuse and toxicity in a marriage is considered normal or tolerated, it becomes the permanent mindset of a person that one must strive to make their relationship work despite the various demeaning and hurtful phases in their married relationship. Please note that making a decision here is a case-by-case situation. I personally have a firm reservation against divorce; however, when a relationship is abusive and toxic, wisdom demands choosing life rather than dying in an unhealthy marriage.

Simple Steps to End an Unhealthy Relationship

The idea of leaving an unhealthy relationship begins an unwanted chain of concerning thoughts that often preoccupy your mind and intensify feelings of fear, dilemma, and anxiety. Ending a toxic relationship can never be easy and quick for a person, as it involves two people with many differences of opinion, hatred, bitterness, and cold-heartedness for each other. A relationship that lacks any care or kindness for one another is not a safer one either. However, seeking divorce can sometimes provoke an adverse reaction from the other side. Thus, one must be cautious when looking for a complete separation, as it could help you have a safe landing from the flight of an unhealthy married relationship that has strived enough to survive the turbulence of toxicity. So, let's learn a few quick and simple steps that can help us implement our plans and thoughts swiftly and smoothly without creating any further problems between the two in a relationship.

Make a Plan

One of the biggest hurdles that come in the way of separation is the last-moment plans and ideas that may change your intentions and entire perception of seeking a divorce. It may be anything, either your dead love trying to breathe in again, your attachment and addiction toward your partner, an intense thought of guilt and remorse, or merely the innocent faces of your children. These factors tie up unbreakable shackles in your feet that restrict you from deciding for peace and liberty. Thus, making the right plan at the right time is the prime requirement, as it prepares you for any uncertainty. Furthermore, it is always better to have a backup plan, as it can help deal with any weird situation that crops up with questions of ifs and buts. Thus, it is a must to have clarity of thought, which ought to be framed sequentially to help you gain a vision that supports you in identifying what to do in any given situation.

Create Financial Independence

Out of many probable reasons, financial dependence is often the biggest one that restricts most women from leaving their toxic partners, especially in cases where the men are the sole breadwinners for their families. Fighting for your happiness and rights becomes a demanding task. With financial independence, one can opt out of a toxic relationship. This situation gets even worse if you have children, as seeking a separation would not only ruin yours but also the lives of your kids. Thus, one must make up one's mind and gather the courage and confidence to stand on their own two feet to gain financial independence, as this is the foremost step when you are looking forward to moving on.

Get Support From Family and Friends

Sometimes, all that you need to get through a difficult time is a shoulder to rely upon to express your heart and weep without the fear of being judged or condemned, which makes you feel energized and uplifted. Often, this helping hand is the most sought-after support and can be anyone in your family or close friends. At times, being with the people who love you unconditionally lets you be who you are and puts you in a comfort zone where you forget all your miseries and problems. Similarly, in the case of dealing with a toxic relationship, it is vital to have your loved ones around you who can become your emotional support and strength in this challenging time of life. These people can help you get out of this toxic relationship and stop turning back to a relationship that fills your life with hurtful and painful memories. Ensure this is a good company, though, with genuine intentions.

Seek Professional Help

Many factors restrict one from opting for divorce despite living in a toxic relationship. At times, the immense love and addiction for your soulmate can compel you to compromise your self-respect and happiness. In such cases, a person is not able to make wise decisions for themselves, as each time they try, they fail and are unable to keep themselves away from their toxic relationship. At times, the trauma and the negativities haunt a person to the core, which can disturb their mental balance. In both circumstances, taking help from a professional like a counselor or therapist could support them in making the right decision.

Distance Yourself From Your Toxic Partner

When you decide to give up on a toxic relationship, it is important to cut off all communication and contact with them. Being in touch with your partner could create doubts and confusion and weaken your decision to get over this relationship. In cases where your life partner may be manipulative, there are increased chances that they could use emotional blackmailing and other ways to lure you back into the same toxic married life. When you build a massive wall between the two of you, it opens the gate to many new opportunities and instances to be happy and build up your empire of happiness all over again.

Required Action Steps

1. Be mindful before making such a big decision, as once you seek a divorce, it may be difficult to reverse it. Count your costs, seek appropriate help, and only take action when you have explored all solutions to fix the toxic relationship.
2. Make up your mind and gather emotional strength, as this is what can help you make it through your difficult time.
3. Have open communication with your children and explain to them that divorce is merely ending a toxic relationship. At the same time,

there is much more to add to one's life and happiness after this.

4. Put in great efforts to keep yourself preoccupied with positive thoughts and people around you who can take you closer to your future goals rather than sobbing at the past and recalling the hurtful memories.

A life partner empowers and compliments you, but if the same person becomes the reason for negativity, threat, and toxicity, then it is better to save your life and move on peacefully. *"The prudent foresees evil and hides, but the simple pass on and are punished."* [1]

---

1. *Proverbs* 22:3

Chapter 9

Overcoming the Shame and Blame Game

> *Know your worth and please don't invest in toxic people or relationships, because any bond that requires servicing is not worth your time.*
>
> — *Masaba Gupta, a Talented Fashion Designer*

Blaming others for an unfortunate event is one of the innate human characteristics that most of us have within us. It is not unusual to find one who questions others as to 'whose fault it was?' No doubt, blaming others for wrongdoing is an easy task that helps us discharge and liberate our inner anger and pain, thereby making us feel more authoritative in negative situations. However, very few of us realize what harm it can do to the other person being blamed, the impact on the relationship, and the engraved marks on the bond between two people. So, let's dive deep and understand what it is and how this shame and blame game begins in a married relationship, which is the most undesirable U-turn on the roads of love within a marriage.

Understanding the Shame and Blame Game

When a couple ties the knot of marriage, they have an unsaid understanding that both partners are equal, which gives them the authority to blame each other for their faults. The major twist in most relationships is that either the partners are right and justified or both are wrong. At the same time, each one of them tries to blame the other one to make themselves feel accomplished and satisfied. However, most of us ignore the harsh impacts it could have on our relationship as each blame game pushes us apart from the other, thus creating an emotional barrier and disconnection. In extreme cases, the blame and shame cycle continues to haunt one even after the married relationship is over, as one keeps blaming the other for the misfortunes. The blame game begins with a feeling of shame when the inner self recognizes that they have done something wrong. They try to manipulate and put the blame on the other person. But even after blaming the other one, the person doesn't even get the empathy that they need the most. Therefore, the birth of the feeling of shame gives rise to the blame game, which gradually becomes a defined part of one's relationship and contributes to growing into a never-ending cycle.

Tips to Break the Shame and Blame Cycle

One of the best ways to eliminate the shame-blame game is to create awareness in one's mind about the initial reactions to sensing a situation, which is the basis for initiating the shame-blame cycle. Identifying the shame triggers is a crucial step to undermine the problem and various aspects that can make you start over this cycle once again, spreading more toxicity in relationships. Further, inculcating a sense of resilience is another significant step that can help one stop blaming others. Apart from this, being vocal and expressive about what triggers the feeling of shame within you can also help solve the conflict of the shame-blame game. Other essential steps can help avoid the shame-blame cycle, which reignites the fire in an inflamed relationship. So, let's explore the simple tips that can help you overcome shame and regret.

End Victimhood

The critical reason that initiates the shame-blame game is the habit of playing the victim in every circumstance. When you develop a perception of blaming others for all the blunders or mistakes rather than holding yourself accountable for the wrong actions, it induces a feeling of shame, ultimately leading to a shame-blame game. The best tactic to avoid this situation is to adopt the habit of taking responsibility for your actions. Similarly, if even after seeking a divorce, one keeps turning the previous pages of their life and continues the blame game, it would simply ruin your future and peace of mind and make you live in guilt or remorse forever. Thus, to move ahead in life, one must adopt the idea of taking responsibility for whatever happened and changed the lives of the two, rather than behaving like a victim and living with pain and sadness till eternity. Everyone is absolutely responsible for the outcome of their lives, and no one is to blame.

Surround Yourself With Positive People

Living with memories of the past is often a cause of aggravating the shame-blame game. Sharing your heartbreak story with a negative person who digs out the worst from a misfortune can end up with you blaming your partner. Thus, it is vital to choose the right type of companion for yourself who can guide and motivate you toward forgetting the bygones, taking a lesson from them, and focusing on your present and future. As they say, one is better alone than sharing ill company; likewise, surrounding yourself with positive people can help you discover the productive aspects of divorce, which support you in moving ahead in life.

Repeat Positive Affirmations

Positive affirmations possess a transformative power that can reshape an individual's perspective. In moments of depression, sorrow, shame, or guilt over past events, diligently repeating positive affirmations can be remarkably beneficial. Phrases like "whatever happened was for the best," or "all things are working together for my good," or "this is not the conclusion of my life, and I will recover my life and secure my destiny" are just a few examples that can assist in dispelling inner guilt and shame, enabling individuals to break free from the cycle of self-blame and self-condemnation. Remember, what you say is what you get. There is power in the spoken word.

. . .

Practice Meditation

Meditation is a powerful technique that helps calm one's mind and body against the storm that keeps going inside one. Dealing with the negativities of divorce can create endless stress, tension, and regrets in one's mind, which holds one haunted now and then. One keeps thinking and overthinking, often blaming oneself and sometimes one's partners, too. However, with meditation, one can quickly reflect on the better perspectives of life. Practicing meditation supports one's ability to be honest about their decisions, opinions, and aspects, which helps in learning from previous mistakes and boosts the ability to concentrate on the positive aspects of life.

Embrace Forgiveness

When one ends up in divorce with one's partner, it brings a whirl of depressing thoughts to one's mind, which is often the result of self-criticism and self-judgment. However, when one focuses on one's emotions and mindfully accepts them as one's fate, it helps switch one's thought process from blame to understanding. Most of the time, one's happiness and peace of mind depend primarily on one's perception and the choices one makes. Thus, choosing self-forgiveness can help improve one's understanding, which is the basis for healing and moving forward.

No doubt, self-forgiveness is hard, but by practicing self-compassion and kindness toward oneself, it becomes easier to accept and overcome the negative thoughts that help to be forgiving toward oneself and others. Self-forgiveness is the key to developing a happy and healthy life, as it not only improves one's emotional and mental well-being but also boosts positivity within one. Creating an optimistic outlook is the key to building stronger and healthier relationships; thus, self-forgiveness is the foundation for reaching the core of tranquility and joy in life.

In the same vein, forgiving one's partner as one moves on is very important; unforgiveness can be a roadblock to other open doors. One should not keep any bitterness against one's partner. One might not be in the relationship again; however, one might still have some related things to do together, especially when children are involved.

Required Action Steps

1. Always think twice before making a significant decision in life so that it leaves no room for any regrets or blame later.

2. Never get influenced by any external factor like your manipulative partner, family, or friends when you are making an important decision in life.

3. Accept your fate and learn lessons from your life rather than wasting your precious time, health, and energy blaming others.

4. Shame-blame game is itself toxic, and living with it could never let you find harmony, so try to change your negative habits.

5. Don't let hatred reside in your heart, even if it is for your toxic partner, as this is the root cause that will never let you live in peace.

Make peace with your past by accepting the bitter truth and moving ahead to shine brightly for yourself and your kids. *"For the path of the just is like a shining light that shines ever brighter unto the perfect day."* [1]

---

1. *Proverbs 4:18*

Chapter 10

Grieving Your Loss

> *In order to reach your highest potential, it is imperative that you remove all negative people from your life.*
>
> — *Germany Kent, an American Broadcaster*

We get into the relationship of marriage with the expectation of living a happy and fun-filled life with the one we love the most. However, at times, things do not go as planned, and life takes a U-turn, which may flip one's world upside down and leave one alone to grieve for a loss. Divorce can be extremely overwhelming, as it causes immense pain, misery, and stressful and unsettling emotions. Divorces are hurtful whether or not they are out of one's own will, as it is not just the end of a married relationship with the one that one loved but the death of the promises that one made to each other, the dreams one had seen together, and the commitment to stand by their side till the last breath, it is normal and obvious for one to grieve the loss of their loved one after the divorce—even if they were not happy with each other because life had opened the gates of uncertainty and drastically changed every sphere of their lives. Divorce is not just two hearts getting apart from each other; instead, it is the death of the emotions, the love, the expectations, and the hopes that not only hamper one's lifestyle but also affect one's children, family, friends, and professional and personal lives.

To bear the pain bestowed by life, some people wear a mask of happiness and peace in front of their peers to show they are satisfied and have moved on. While some may grieve deeply to the extent that they ruin their future hopes and the probability of living happily once again. However, grieving is a crucial phase in the life of a person once they have ended their relationship, as it helps one completely get over their pain and shattering loss. At the same time, it is crucial to understand that grieving is a coping and healing strategy that helps one move forward. So, let's explore the various stages of grieving, their importance, and the different tips to get over these emotions healthily.

Stages of Grieving a Break-up

Grieving over one's broken relationship is not only a painful and challenging task but can also sometimes cause loneliness, leading to social isolation. Isolation happens not only because one is grieving and wants to be alone in this journey of life but also because sometimes society, family, and friends are likely to show no care or support. This happens not because they don't care about one but because they may not understand the stages of grieving one may be going through and how to offer help. This lack of validation from family, friends, and other relatives may compel one to experience disenfranchised grief. Disenfranchised grief is a situation in the coping period that is not openly acknowledged, supported, or mourned by others in society. In such scenarios, one must get out of their isolated zones and talk directly with family and friends that they are in urgent need of emotional support and need help. In this entire path of grieving the end of a married relationship, there is nothing to be judged as right or wrong; instead, it is a process that goes through five clear stages. So, let's explore the various stages of grieving that may not necessarily happen in the same order for different individuals. Still, it is fundamental to get out of the shackles of the memories, pain, anxiety, and aggression of the past unhealthy relationship.

Desperateness for Answers

Once one makes the decision to separate from one's partner and knows that divorce is inevitable, one enters the stage where the desperation to uncover all the hidden aspects of one's unhealthy relationship is so intense that it occupies one's mind totally. Initially, one may feel sudden cramps of anxiety when one's mind is filled with different sorts of grilling questions that keep hovering in one's head in search of answers and hold one back from moving ahead in life. Innumerable questions like "Why did the divorce happen?", "Was this the only best solution to the situation?" "Did I deserve this in my life?" "Where did I go wrong in understanding my partner?"

Gradually, without realizing anything, one enters a stage where one feels overwhelmed in search of the prospective reasons why one's spouse cheated on one or tortured one in the relationship. In the struggle to find the voids in their harsh actions, one often begins to believe that one's relationship deserves one more chance and can strive through all the storms. This entire process can be very exhausting, which not only entails one's thoughts but also becomes embarrassing when one begins to explore and search for justifications from everyone one meets, whether it is one's family, friends, office colleagues, or merely strangers passing. All one begins to look for is a convincing word of sympathy that whatever happened was not right, and one must give one's relationship another try. However, all this is merely a natural response to one's defensive psychology, which acts as a shield to keep one away from the reality of one's life and can comfort one by easing the pain, fear, and disappointment.

Denial

This is the stage where one's heart takes control of one's emotions and thoughts, and more than one's mind knows about the truth. When one is aware that one has lost one's loved one, one's heart doesn't allow one to believe it completely. The denial stage, as the name signifies, emphasizes a phase in which the person has some hope deep down in their heart that things could be reversed and that they may once again reunite with their separated partner. More often, during this stage, one has a hidden expectation and desire that there exists a ray of hope that can make a way out of this depressing situation and that things could become as before.

The denial stage is not something that can make one go psycho about the entire event; instead, it is a vital defense mechanism that prepares one to face the facts and is an easy way to lower the intensity of the whole situation. Gradually, when one moves out of the denial stage, they begin to realize the pains they have been trying to avoid all this time. The end of this stage could be more challenging to handle as it confronts one with the painful reality of life.

Bargaining

The bargaining stage is another defensive mechanism, like the denial stage. When a person is in the bargaining stage, they do varied things, like pleasing their ex or leaving no stone unturned to save their broken relationship. Sometimes, a partner may try to negotiate with their ex that they will change their behaviors, make promises in the name of their children, or try to calm their mind in the name of their family and future commitments.

Simply put, the bargaining stage is the most vulnerable phase of grieving, making one helpless. The intense rush of emotions throughout one's mind and body makes one feel numb enough to accept the harsh truth that nothing can change the situation. Although a voice at the back of one's mind consistently urges 'if only' and 'what if' statements that bring back some hope in one's life. Bargaining is a helpful stage in the grieving process as it helps postpone the negative emotions of confusion, anxiety, sadness, hurt, and stress.

Relapse

Relapse is a stage where one is scared to face one's fears and is not willing to imagine the unnamed and incomplete life that would happen without one's soulmate. It is a phase that directs a relationship toward reconciliation for peace and to avoid hardships. Somehow, one cries, begs or convinces one's ex to give the relationship another try. However, with lots of discomfort, insecurities, and sacrifices, one may alone try to drag the weight of a dead relationship, which ultimately results in separation once again. Once two hearts are disconnected from each other, it can be very challenging for the two to get back together, except by some divine interventions.

Anger

Unlike the denial phase, which is a coping or defense mechanism, anger is a masking strategy. When a person ends up in a permanent separation from their loved one, it is obvious to feel the pain and fear of losing them. However, not everyone is brave enough to accept this fact of life. Some people try to conceal this flow of negative emotions by showing a higher intensity of anger and furious behavior. Most of the time, showing anger at every other person they meet up with and creating issues becomes an involuntary action of the brain to fight against the hidden emotions of frustration, sadness, betrayal, and rage within oneself.

One may show anger at their separated partner, themselves, and that period that destroyed their peace of mind. Believing that anger is more of a survival stage could boost morale and help with early healing. It would help one feel that anger is a normal feeling, which could make it easier for them to accept it, name it, feel it, and let it happen. The anger stage is crucial as it helps one stay alive and endure the dangers. Feeling angry in the middle of painful emotions helps strengthen one by protecting one from reaching the breakdown stage and feeling pity for oneself. This should be, however, adequately managed so as not to degenerate into another danger.

Initial Acceptance

As the name implies, this stage makes one believe the truth and eases the process of making peace with the past. Entering this stage marks the onset of thoughts and a strong mindset that one has accepted that the divorce has occurred. This is the time when one starts being kind toward oneself and thinking about how that could help one liberate all the pain, anxiety, and fear one has been living with all this time. It is more of a refreshing stage in one's life where one decides to live again and not let the past hinder the path of life. This stage may not bring immediate happiness, harmony, and flourishing, but it is the beginning of a better tomorrow. One learns to face one's sad emotions and how to uplift one's mind and life simultaneously. However, some people may feel that they would never be able to overcome this loss and would struggle for the rest of their lives with hurtful and painful memories. It simply means that they are still far away from entering the peaceful acceptance phase and may still be in an earlier phase.

Healing is a gradual and slow process that may take time to happen. The best way to eliminate the sad emotions and negativities is to give oneself enough time to grieve the loss until one is exhausted by these churning emotions. Once one gets through all the stages of grieving, one can move forward in life with the feeling that bygones are bygones and everything wrong is done and dusted, which marks the onset of a new and beautiful beginning in one's life.

Redirected Hope

When one's marriage is over, it begins a turmoil of emotions within oneself that creates sadness, anger, anxiety, and confusion, which marks the death of that single vital factor that is crucial for the existence of life's hope. It's natural and normal for one to feel immense hopelessness, as divorce has shattered every single dream, wish, and future that one had ever imagined for oneself with one's lost partner. However, as they say, after every dark and depressing sunset, there is a brighter and more sunrise. Similarly, in the life of everyone who has fought for their happiness, peace, rights, and self-respect within their toxic marriage, a ray of hope appears when the thunder of storms has passed, opening the gate for new horizons to shine and light up one's life with beautiful colors.

After the acceptance phase, when one has shaken one's hands with one's destiny, it is time to think about oneself again, getting into the race of life. Redirected hope is a stage that helps to teach the sense of positivity, courage, and strength to live once again and fight one's battle all alone without feeling weak and taking pity on oneself. We all have some reserves of hope locked into a box hidden within ourselves, which we only dig out and explore when we have grieved a significant loss.

Allow Yourself to Grieve

Dealing with unwelcoming emotions after a divorce is not an easy task, as sometimes the negative, depressing, and painful feelings are so intense that it may take a long time for one to completely recover. Grieving is a natural phenomenon that happens after a person has faced heartbreak in a married relationship and evokes emotions like anger, sadness, loneliness, and crying. Often, these emotions are considered harmful and unkind gestures, condemned by many. Thus, sometimes people try to conceal their anger; however, they forget that when one fills oneself with anger, it might take the form of dangerous emotions like arrogance, irritation, and frustration. However, many people smile after a loss. The secret behind this smile is that they have shared their trauma and suffering with their loved ones, which helped fade away the dark fog of pain, fear, and anxiety that has shown up in front of their eyes after a divorce.

There are many ways of venting one's anger, like expressing one's feelings with someone close or even crying. However, for some people, crying may be a sign of weakness. But even the strongest person can cry, as it is just a way to vent one's emotions. Sometimes, when one shares one's heartbroken feelings with one's loved ones, there are chances that one cannot balance one's emotions, which triple down in the form of tears. Once one cries and expresses one's feelings, it arouses the belief that one is empowered and liberated by letting go of all the negativity in one's life. Thus, crying is one of the best healing emotions that helps in venting out oneself, as it releases endorphins and oxytocin, which improves the mood and makes one feel better.

Do's and Don'ts of Grieving a Broken Relationship

Grieving over the loss is an integral part of healing oneself from the trauma and anxiety that one has faced

after an unsuccessful relationship. However, overcoming these draining emotions can be a daunting task
if one gets stuck in the cycle of these negative feelings.
Thus, the following do's and don'ts can help one practice self-care and become a more robust version of
oneself.

1. Accept the situation and move on rather than
   contemplating the past, trying to dig out one's
   mistakes, or feeling guilty about the entire
   situation. The more one obsesses over the
   broken relationship, the more it will haunt and
   exhaust the positive energy, allowing one to
   move forward.

2. Never try to suppress or condemn your
   grieving emotions, thinking that they may
   remind you of the past and hinder your mental
   peace. Instead, emotions like anger, fear,
   resentment, sadness, and confusion are all
   essential parts of the grieving process that help
   make one feel better and ease this phase of life.

3. Treat yourself with love, kindness, and
   compassion, which directly improves your self-
   worth and self-confidence to move ahead in
   life. More often, in such situations, one begins

to initiate a self-blame game, which ultimately kills one's energy and enthusiasm to look at life again with an optimistic outlook.

4. Never try to isolate yourself by concealing your emotions in front of your family and friends. Instead, express your feelings to loved ones who would support you in your grieving journey. Talking about the turmoil of emotions could keep you from feeling lonely and stressed and ease the healing process.

5. Keep yourself busy by focusing more on the positive and better aspects of life, like your children, family, friends, and professional life. Living more in the present could help you to think about the positive aspects of life and minimize the temptation to contact your ex.

6. Never be confined to that same physical space that could remind you of the hard times and the broken relationship. Instead, try to transform and redesign your personal space, which could reset your emotional and mental status. The more you close the doors of your memories, the more it opens the gate toward new endeavors and happiness.

Required Action Steps

1. Feel free to share your grief with your close family and friends, as they can significantly help.

2. Never feel embarrassed or uneasy about crying when you feel like doing so, as it can help you vent out all your inner negativities, making you feel relaxed and calm.

3. Don't hold yourself down for anything wrong in your life, as it can make you fall prey to guilt and shame that will never let you grieve your past.

4. Keep all the things away that remind you of your traumatic past, your unfriendly spouse, and your unhealthy marital relationship, as they will act as constraints on your feet and will stop you from moving ahead in life.

5. Divert your attention by engaging yourself in rediscovering your true self and for the welfare of your children, as it can act as a motivating force in your life.

Life never has shortcuts for everything, and, indeed, painful times are often more daunting. As there is always a ray of hope after every dark night, likewise, after the end of an unhealthy relationship, there is always a scope for getting started in a new way, with a new spirit, with a new companion, but on better terms. *"For there is hope for a tree, if it is cut down, that it will sprout again."* [1]

---

1. *Job* 14:7

Chapter 11

Move Toward the Road to Healing

> Losing will not always amount to a loss, sometimes you have to lose those toxic relationships and bad habits to create a space for better things.

— *Gift Gugu Mona, a Transformational Speaker*

It is very natural and normal for one to feel lousy when they have been a victim of abuse and domestic violence in a toxic relationship. In such a scenario, the road toward healing and recovery might seem like a difficult task, and it can possibly take a long time to overcome the trauma and pain of the afflictions. Anyone who has gone through so many physical and psychological tortures by their loved one may have many fears, tensions, grudges, guilt, and questions that may make their days and nights a big challenge. Getting worried and running away from all these is not the ultimate solution. Instead, one needs to gather all their courage and energy to face reality and give a hard blow to these negativities by exhibiting the guts to move forward in life.

Tips to Move Toward Rediscovering Your True Self

Even after fighting and winning against one's life partner, one has a long way to go toward healing the deep wounds. There are many different and exciting ways to divert oneself from the bad memories and make one's journey toward rediscovering one's better self effective. Here, we have many such activities that one should try to move ahead in life in a productive manner, which can make them healthier and happier again.

Prepare Yourself to Accept Help and Support

The first and most important thing that can help one recover from past trauma is one's perception. Many times, when one is afflicted by some mishap in life, one tends to narrow one's vision and start thinking like everyone around. By so doing, one categorizes all friends and foes in the same queue, often making one's surroundings toxic. In such a pessimistic situation, it becomes almost impossible to ask for help or accept assistance from well-wishers. In this way, one's negative mindset compels one to think that everyone who is approaching one for rescue is either trying to mock or is rubbing salt in one's wounds. To overcome this, one should build a positive mindset by practicing meditation, repeating positive affirmations, and even seeking the help of a counselor in the most challenging situations. Thus, one must always try to keep one's vision clear and broad by welcoming the support offered by others in difficult times, which can make the journey toward healing easier and shorter.

Spare Time to Care for Yourself

After a long and tiring journey of struggling for survival, one may feel very vulnerable and disinterested in life. The different phases of these traumatic events in one's life can trigger negative feelings of low self-esteem, self-doubt, and remorse that can create hatred for oneself. During such times of hardship, one must always pay attention to the signs that the body shows, depicting a need for self-care. Sparing some quality time, especially for oneself, becomes the need of the hour to deal with the growing pessimism within one's mind. These foul feelings push one toward situations in which they can become a reason for self-harm. Thus, one should establish a fixed routine, including ample time for pampering oneself. There are many simple and interesting ways— like watching a stress-relieving movie or concert, listening to soothing music, spending time with nature and pets, focusing on grooming oneself or engaging in some social or religious activities—that can change one's life toward achieving a better self.

Focus On Feeding Your Soul Too

Along with caring for one's body, it is also important to look after the healing of one's soul, which represents one's true identity. Very often, a smile on our faces gives rise to the false notion that we are satisfied with our lives and everything happening around us. But reality is not always what we see, and we fail to understand the hidden pains and agonies of our souls. While facing the torture of a violent partner in a toxic relationship, the soul of an individual gets injured, and one gives up any hope of living a happy and peaceful life. It is necessary to know oneself in the best possible manner to revive one's soul and stand firm, which demands focus on one's inner strengths and weaknesses. Thus, working on nourishing one's soul by practicing positive self-talk, embracing spirituality, and forgiving others and ourselves is one crucial step that can help in the healing process.

Don't Look Back and Regret Ever

One of the golden rules one needs to follow while recovering from unpleasant memories is to never look back and feel guilty for what has happened. In life, there are many situations where one must become very strong and make harsh decisions that may change one's life forever. Reflecting on one's life events and learning from one's mistakes is something entirely different from sobbing over the past, which will never let one move ahead in life. Another critical aspect that can help in healing one's wounds is forgiving one's ex-partner, as it will help one forget the hurtful memories associated with one's toxic married relationship. Thus, accepting the truth of one's life and letting things and people go without a wrinkle on one's forehead needs a strong heart and an altruistic personality, which can carve out the path toward healing and help restart one's life again.

Required Action Steps

1. Recollect all your strengths and curb your negativities.
2. Always try to learn from your mistakes instead of sobbing over them.
3. Never look back to regret your past mistakes.
4. Maintain an optimistic mindset to continue moving forward.
5. Work regularly to empower and reenergize your soul.

Life is a challenging journey for everyone, but adhering to the above steps can facilitate a smoother, more straightforward, and happier transition toward a new beginning. *"A merry heart does good, like medicine, but a broken spirit dries the bones."* [1]

---

1. *Proverbs 17:22*

Chapter 12

Ways to Avoid Unhealthy Relationships in the Future

> *Toxic people attach themselves like cinder blocks tied to your ankles, and then invite you for a swim in their poisoned waters.*
>
> — *John Mark Green, a Passionate Writer*

Choosing a life partner is one of the most important and risky decisions, as it is fundamental for building a happy and healthy lifestyle in the future. A soulmate is the one who becomes your support and stands by your side through the thick and thin of life. We try to choose the best partner for ourselves, someone who can complement and accept us just as we are. We land on the island of marriage with the hope and vision that it will brighten our future and fill our world with contentment, success, and tranquility. However, when these life decisions go wrong, it can make us feel like we are sailing in a drowning ship with no ray of hope on either side. Being in such a relationship can be overwhelming, arouses negative emotions, and makes one feel like the end of the world. Some people gather courage and recollect themselves all over again, believing it was merely a game of destiny, and decide to give life another chance. Getting disheartened and losing hope because of the past toxic relationship is not the solution; instead, one must begin all over again to achieve one's part of happiness and move forward in life with new hope and positivity.

Don'ts While Making a New Relationship

It is imperative to figure out ways to help save oneself from committing similar mistakes again and ending up in a toxic relationship. So, let's look at the various things one should avoid, which can help one build a healthy relationship by assessing whether one's partner is toxic.

Never Rush Your Time to Know the Other Person

It's a common human trait that once one has tasted betrayal, harassment, or a toxic relationship, one would be conscious before repeating the same mistake. Taking lessons from one's sinking and depressing experiences can help one avoid future obstacles by not becoming the prey of the same torturous life again. Thus, to escape the negativity, one must take enough time to understand their dating partner before marrying them. Some of the tips for knowing and exploring compatibility with one's new partner are:

1. The foremost and easiest way is to self-analyze how you feel when you are with them. Suppose their company makes you feel ugly, boring, ashamed, inferior, discouraged, and inadequate. In that case, they are unhealthy for you and would be toxic. However, if their presence empowers you with confidence, self-worth, and positivity, then being in a long-term relationship would be a healthy choice. The right soulmate would always make you feel comfortable just like you are, with no obligations, self-consciousness, comments, or corrections.

2. Sometimes, some people enter our lives like a blessing, helping us to dig out the best in ourselves and making us feel more capable, engaging, and intelligent. On the other hand, if

your dating partner tries to highlight the less pleasant traits and aspects of your personality, then it's time to say goodbye and move forward.

3. It is essential to ask yourself if the new partner makes you feel worse, better, or the same as before. A genuine partner would make you feel liberated and fill you with lots of energy, hope, and zeal to achieve your desired goals in life; while getting together with the wrong partner would make you feel exhausted and drained as they suck out the life and positivity from within you. Sometimes, a partner may devalue you by cracking humiliating jokes and making sarcastic comments in a fun way, making you feel worse about yourself.

4. If being in the company of your dating partner escalates the creative side within you and inspires you to do new and better things in life, then they are a gem that can add value to your life and help you find peace, solace, and happiness.

5. The right soulmate pushes you toward doing productive things, whether grooming yourself, doing workouts, practicing meditation to improve your physical and mental health, or growing spiritually. Therefore, it becomes easy

to differentiate between a healthy and a toxic relationship merely by the activities they push you to do together.

Never Ignore the Red Flags

Relationships are an integral part of human existence that help one socialize, form connections, and improve mental health. However, not all relationships do that; some may be toxic enough to destroy one's peace of mind and ruin one's life. One such meaningful connection is the married relationship, which is the most intimate and impactful in one's life. While getting into the wrong relationship can threaten happiness and tranquility, recognizing and understanding the red flags is one of the most innovative ways to avoid a toxic relationship and prevent future complications and pain. Red flags are the signs and warnings that can help identify your dating partner's manipulative and unhealthy attitude. However, red flags sometimes need to be clarified, especially in the initial days of knowing each other. Red flags tend to grow bigger and worsen with time and can take varied forms, like narcissism, aggression, victimization, or abusive behavior. Therefore, when encountering red flags in your dating relationship, you must pause and reflect if you want to continue with them, as sometimes accepting this red flag as a part of your personality could make you suffer later. So, let's delve deep and identify the red flags that are clear signs of saying 'no' to a relationship.

1. When your dating partner exhibits overly controlled behavior that suppresses your own will.
2. When there is no trust between the two of you.
3. When someone special does not make you feel special, it often degrades your self-esteem and breaks you down rather than builds you up.
4. When they exhibit any abusive behavior, be it emotional, physical, or mental.
5. When a person is a victim of substance abuse, it indicates that they are struggling with self-destructive habits and impulse control.
6. When one has narcissistic personality disorder, they may show self-obsessed behavior, which indicates that they care more for themselves than their partner's desires and happiness.
7. When your dating partner faces anger management issues, it may be a sign that they lose their temper and lack emotional regulation, which may be threatening to their significant other.

8. When a person shows signs of codependency. A partner with a codependent attitude could burden the relationship by increasing the mental load and exhausting you emotionally.

9. When you face extreme difficulties resolving conflicts with your would-be partner, it indicates that you lack compatibility and there is no chance of getting into a constructive conflict, which is significant for a healthy relationship.

10. When your dating partner has constant problems and jealousy each time you mingle with other social relationships, like family and friends, it portrays their selfish attitude as they consider their happiness over yours.

11. When an individual exhibits gaslighting, which is an emotionally abusive and manipulative tactic. It can be considered a clear indication of a red flag in a relationship.

12. When someone lacks emotional intelligence. Such a person can never empathize with you or understand your feelings, which marks a red flag.

Never Let Uncertainty Sway Your Mind

The innate human nature compels one to crave security in every sphere of life; however, uncertainty forms an integral part of our world and arouses anxiety, stress, and worry. When a person has a bitter experience in a past married relationship, they become more conscious, aware, and skeptical about making the same decision again while looking for a prospective life partner. In this endeavor of life, sometimes one may feel uncertain about their dating partner, which makes them unsure about getting into a married relationship. However, having any uncertainty may ingrain extreme emotions of fear, anxiety, stress, and negative perception toward their partner, eventually resulting in future problems, arguments, conflicts, and toxicity in relationships. Thus, it's crucial to choose a relationship that doesn't have any mixed feelings associated with it to gain maximum satisfaction, contentment, and happiness. So, here is a list of common mistakes often made either consciously or unconsciously but can bring some form of regret.

1. Often, when a person has set their frame of mind as to what type of partner they wish to have regarding looks, health, personality, qualification, or status, there is a higher chance of choosing the wrong partner. However, when one decides to be open-minded about one's

choices and perceptions while looking for a partner, one may be fortunate enough to find someone who is highly compatible, understanding, trustworthy, and has a solid emotional connection.

2. Most people believe love is the most crucial prerequisite for a happy married life. However, the fire of love and passion for each other diminishes. Eventually, it vanishes without adequate commitment as married life progresses forward. Therefore, looking for other signs that could help guide your relationship toward happiness and peace is better. Being in a relationship with an individual who is a friend, shares some common interests and goals, and exhibits trust, humility, and respect toward you can result in a strong, committed, and long-term bond.

3. Most people decide to marry someone they believe they are deeply and madly in love with and that life would be incomplete without them while ignoring the other vital signs crucial for a successful marriage. They should instead open their eyes to the truth and look forward to settling for someone who adds love

and great value to their life, happiness, and peace.

4. Manipulation is a clear sign of a lack of trust between partners, gradually letting uncertainty creep into the relationship. Suppose you feel that your dating partner is playing manipulative games to take control over you and make you feel like a puppet; it is time to bid goodbye and move ahead.

5. The most essential part of getting into a relationship is listening to what your heart and mind say about your dating partner. Exploring your inner self would give you the correct answer as to whether your feelings about your dating partner are right. Therefore, one must always trust their instincts while making important life decisions, as it leaves no space for uncertainties to fill in the voids and create further confusion.

Required Action Steps

1. Listen to your instincts, intuitions, and spirit, but always use your mind and intelligence to judge your partner wisely.

2. Spend time getting to know and exploring your would-be partner before committing to a relationship.

3. Never hide any details or information about your past from the dating partner, as it may sow seeds of mistrust.

4. Be alert for any warning signs that you notice in the behavior and attitude of your new dating partner.

5. Discuss your would-be partner's habits and behavioral patterns with a trusted friend or counselor to ensure your decision.

6. Do not hesitate to seek divine guidance and spiritual counseling.

Finding a life partner who could be called your better half and become a bolster in your life is a challenging task. However, with a few mindful acts and a sincere perspective, one can easily focus on achieving a healthy relationship in the future. *"There is a way that seems right to a man, but its end is the way of death."* [1]

---

1. *Proverbs 14:12; 16:25*

Chapter 13

Inspirational Stories of Marriages Saved from Divorce

> *A great marriage is not when the 'perfect couple' comes together. It is when an imperfect couple learns to enjoy their differences.*
>
> — *Dave Meurer, an Award-Winning Writer*

When life throws complex challenges before us, we often feel broken and upset with life, which can also make us stand alone in this crowded world. Many times, to get rid of the existing problems and challenges of a toxic marriage, we end up inviting new and much bigger issues. However, it seems very easy to stay away and imagine one's life without one's spouse, but the truth is far more bitter than we imagine. In our busy lives, we often fail to understand the real meaning and purpose of wedlock and become victims of toxicity in a relationship due to many unexpected and unwanted reasons. Most people choose to break up the bond with their spouse instead of giving them a second chance to recreate and rejuvenate their love and passion. In such a depressing and hurting phase of life, looking at people who have moved toward positivity in their relationships by adopting patience, forgiveness, and compassion gives us immense motivation and direction to improve things rather than quit. So, let's turn the pages of the lives of a few inspirational celebrities who have set live examples of reliving their relationships by reconciling their thoughts, ideas, ambitions, and emotions.

Victoria Beckham and David Beckham

Ever since the love hormones begin to show up, we start dreaming of a married life that is a perfect blend of love, trust, respect, understanding, and togetherness, wishing it to last forever. David and Victoria Beckham are admirable married couples who never fail to astonish us with their shared bond and pure love for each other. Being one of the longest-standing Hollywood couples who never left their partner's side through thick and thin of life, they believe that their eternal and unconditional love for each other has helped them make it through 24 years in wedlock. The parents of four exceptional children have been through rumors of infidelity and divorce several times. However, their reliance on each other in every struggle saved their marriage.

The couple claimed keeping the spark and love alive in a long marriage was never easy. However, the values, willingness of togetherness, and, most importantly, having an amazing understanding of each other made marriage work for them (Staff, 2023). Every marriage is sometimes difficult, filled with innumerable misunderstandings, clashes of interests, differences of opinion, and life choices. Although looking at the exemplary love story of these twosomes, we must believe that no fairytale is perfect. The determination and willpower of a couple to strive together during their journey through life, which is often filled with road bumps, makes an ideal marriage. Thus, the story of David and Victoria Beckham proves that love, at first sight, may happen to anyone, but to make it last forever, one truly needs to devote efforts to developing strong communication, connection, compromise, and commitment.

Jessica Biel and Justin Timberlake

A famous saying emphasizes that everything good does not necessarily come with ease. The same applies when we think about true love and a perfect companion. A dedicated partner would not miss a chance to stand by your side, no matter what happens. Jessica Biel and Justin Timberlake are a fascinating yet ideal couple who have stayed together for over a decade. Their love story, which later turned into a magical marriage, is a living example that when two souls are committed to each other, they are meant to be united in an everlasting bond called marriage. This incredible couple had survived several complicated phases in their relationship even before they married when the rumors of their breakup stole the limelight. However, they supported each other during difficult times and decided to stay silent on their relationship status.

Eventually, their love for each other was revealed to the world when they tied the knot and united beautifully in wedlock. However, as no love story is ideal, so was this one, and destiny tested their love once again with the harsh allegations of infidelity and cheating on Justin Timberlake that broke the headlines. But the couple once again proved the world wrong with their love, togetherness, understanding, loyalty, and honesty toward each other, dismissing every rumor as fake. Justin Timberlake took a firm stand, publicly clarified the matter as a misunderstanding, and apologized to his family and fans for what had happened (Lutkin, 2023). This amazing couple has won many hearts by teaching us life's most important lessons: that every marriage meets failures, disappointments, and trust issues at some phase of the relationship, but when you decide not to give up on your partner, no power can pull you apart.

Kristen Bell and Dax Shepard

It is almost hard to imagine that a couple who have had extensive fights ever since the beginning of their dating time could ever land into a happily married life. They say when love is true, it always finds its way out, and this is so true for Kristen Bell and Dax Shepard, who have enjoyed each other's company as a married couple for the last ten years with their two darling children. This couple didn't fall for each other at first sight because they have expressed themselves as having different personalities. Despite being poles apart, Kristen Bell was full of life and positive energy, whose presence could spread enough happiness and liveliness. In contrast, Dax Shepard exhibited a calm and composed

personality during their early dating. However, sometimes couples who are way too different from each other
tend to attract each other's souls quite firmly, as was the
case in their relationship.

After experiencing several dates on and off, the couple
finally decided to get engaged, successfully leading them
toward tying the knot. Having extremely heated arguments and conflicts was a constant part of their
marriage, but perhaps it only happened because the
couple truly and madly loved each other. However, as
every relationship sometimes gets trapped in tough
times, so does theirs. Still, the couple did not give up and
decided to get help by opting for various therapies that
worked out for them (Kreienberg, 2022). Although this
was not the end, Dax Shepard faced allegations of
cheating on his wife, which he denied on a social media
platform. The two's happy and prosperous married life
is an example for those who believe that having opposite
personalities, having differences of opinion, and getting
into repeated fights are red flags that must be avoided in
a relationship. Instead, the love for each other and the
obsession to stay together for a lifetime are the driving
forces that keep a marriage going.

Jillian Fink and Patrick Dempsey

There is an old fairy tale belief that a love that can stand the test of time is real, while it is pretty surreal for us to accept it. However, going beyond our imaginations, the married relationship of Jillian Dempsey and Patrick Dempsey is an astounding example that finding and keeping a true partner is not a matter of chance; instead, it results from mutual efforts and willingness to be with your partner. However, it was a second marriage, Patrick Dempsey, but once they were together, it seemed to be a perfect bond and companionship for each other. However, a few years later, after their three children, the relationship of this beautiful couple went through difficult times, to the extent that Jillian Dempsey even filed for divorce. Later, the couple confessed that they were not ready to live apart and decided to seek help and opt for couple therapy (Gurung, 2022). This eventually resolved the matter for them and reunited them with even more love, respect, mutual understanding, intimacy, and eagerness to be with each other. The love story of Jillian Dempsey and Patrick Dempsey is no less than a perfect Hollywood movie, wherein no force could separate the couple from each other. The marriage timeline of this fascinating couple makes us believe that if partners exhibit the willingness to strive through difficult times, nothing can stop them from being together.

Required Action Steps

1. One should aim to save their marriage by looking for areas for improvement in the relationship.
2. Adopting simple steps like forgiving your partner, accepting their personality, and expressing love and compassion can make a tremendous difference in mending the relationship.
3. Communication is the key to sorting out all life issues, as it helps understand each other's emotions, desires, and needs, which can make a relationship run smoothly and happily.
4. Every element of life must be well-balanced, whether it be the professional front, friend circle, ambitions, or love life, as it helps provide clarity and improve focus toward achieving a healthy and happy relationship.
5. Having trust and respect in the relationship makes it more robust. It makes it last longer, so set healthy boundaries and give space to your

spouse to let them explore and enjoy the relationship.

No doubt marriages are made in heaven, but we mortals do have to put in some effort to beautify and make every moment of this devout relationship memorable and full of life. *"Let your fountain be blessed, and rejoice with the wife of your youth. As a loving deer and a graceful doe, let her breasts satisfy you at all times; And always be enraptured with her love"* [1]

KEEPING THE FLAME BURNING

Now that you've equipped yourself with the tools to gain Freedom From Unhealthy Relationships, it's time to share the wealth and guide others to the same transformative journey.

By sharing your honest thoughts on Amazon, you're not just leaving a review; you're illuminating the path for other Couples or Singles in relationships seeking the information and empowerment found in Freedom From Unhealthy Relationships.

Your voice matters, and your review can be the guiding light someone needs to embark on their journey to freedom.

Thank you for being a part of this movement. Freedom From Unhealthy Relationships thrives when we pass on our knowledge, and you play a crucial role in that process.

Click here or Scan the QR Code to leave your review on Amazon:

https://www.amazon.com/review/review-your-purchases/?asin=1962758001

SCAN TO REVIEW

---

1. *Proverbs 5:18-19*

Epilogue

As we conclude *Freedom from Unhealthy Relationships*, I want to express my gratitude for taking this journey toward building strong and lasting bonds, resolving conflicts, improving intimacy, and overcoming codependency. This book was carefully researched and written to meet the diverse needs of individuals, transcending religious affiliations, cultural backgrounds, races, and more. Its principles are universal and intended for anyone seeking healthier, happier, and fulfilling relationships.

It is crucial to acknowledge that relationships, by their very nature, require effort and commitment in spite of all odds. In this guide, the emphasis has been on personal responsibility — recognizing that each one has roles to play in maintaining healthy relationships. Choices matter, and the consequences of our actions or inactions are ours to bear.

The approach taken in this book deliberately steers away from relying solely on divine intervention. Instead, it encourages individuals to actively participate in creating the relationships they desire. A saying goes, *"God will not do what He can until we do what we need to do."* This statement encapsulates the essence of our journey — that while faith and divine help are powerful, they are not a substitute for our responsibility.

In the same vein, *"Any faith that makes God responsible for the outcome of one's life is an irresponsible faith."* These words remind us that we must not abdicate our responsibility in the belief that divine intervention will absolve us of the need for personal commitment.

However, having taken the necessary steps and embraced personal responsibility, we must also acknowledge the inevitability of divine possibility and intervention for those who have faith in God. This statement is not a contradiction but a complementary understanding — a recognition that while we strive for the best, we humbly accept that some aspects are beyond our control.

For those seeking a deeper exploration of engaging the power of God for divine intervention, I invite you to explore my other book, ***"God of Wonders."*** This book delves into the spiritual dimensions of life, offering insights into the mysteries of faith and the extraordinary possibilities that unfold when we align our actions with divine principles.

In conclusion, let the wisdom gained from the pages of this book serve as a compass, directing you towards relationships that are not only fulfilling and enriching but also inherently healthy. Recognize that the complexities of relationships are not obstacles but opportunities for growth and understanding.

May you find resilience in your efforts, knowing that every step taken contributes to the tapestry of your connections. Be rest assured that amidst the challenges, wonders can and will unfold in your life. The journey does not conclude with the last page; it extends into the unfolding chapters of your personal relationships. May you continue to navigate with courage, compassion, and a deep-seated conviction that the best is yet to come.

"For whatsoever is born of God overcometh the world: and this is the victory that overcometh the world, even our faith."[1]

---

1.   1 John 5:4

Glossary

1. **Adrenaline**: It is a feeling of stimulation, excitement, and enhanced physical ability as the body produces larger amounts of adrenaline when you are exposed to any type of induced or perceived stress.

2. **Bad Wolf**: It is regarded as something or someone who is held accountable for creating all the problems and complications in a situation; it is used to denote negative qualities within a person.

3. **Blame Game**: An unhealthy environment or a situation in which a person tries to blame an unfortunate event or happening on another person rather than finding a solution or calming the matter.

4. **Bolster**: It is a gesture or an act of kindness and courage that can act as a supporting element to boost strength.

5. **Cakewalk**: A situation or victory that is very easy for one to achieve.

6. **Coercion**: Using intimidation or forceful activities to get your work done by someone.

7. **Construe**: The ability to decode or understand the actions or words of another person in a particular manner; to interpret someone's actions or statement.

8. **Cortisol**: A hormone secreted by the adrenal glands in response to a stressful situation.

9. **Disenfranchised Grief**: It is the grieving phase that is not supported by society and the other family members, and this lack of emotional support prolongs their painful grieving.

10. **Dysfunction**: The inability of a person to portray healthy and sound behavior in society.

11. **Endorphins**: These are the hormones that are released from the body when you are in a stressful or painful situation.

12. **Feeding Your Soul**: An act of making yourself feel at ease and at peace when you are

in the middle of a challenging situation or when things are going well.

13. **Guilt Trip**: A manipulative tactic where a person tries to make someone feel remorseful, guilty, and regretful about their choices, decisions, or actions.

14. **Hallucination**: Consistently experiencing a false perception of an act or happening that does not exist in reality.

15. **Impulsive Behavior**: An instant way of dealing with people or situations without thinking about the later consequences, for instance, using anger, violence, or showing temper.

16. **Marital Rape**: Engaging in an act of sexual intercourse with one's spouse without their consent.

17. **Mindfulness Meditation**: A meditation technique in which you are completely aware of the feelings and sensations of what you are doing at that moment without fear of being judged or interpreted by someone.

18. **Nagging Behavior**: A displeasing behavior that continuously makes someone feel uncomfortable, worried, or insecure.

19. **Narcissistic**: An act or feeling of exaggerating or highlighting one's importance and achievement; showing an extreme interest in and admiration for oneself.

20. **Narcissistic Personality Disorder**: A mental disorder in which a person needs much attention, importance, and admiration, which diminishes their sense of caring for or understanding others.

21. **Nerve of Steel**: An inner characteristic of a person that allows them to maintain their calm and courage in an extremely challenging situation.

22. **Oxytocin**: A hormone produced inside the body that is responsible for managing the major functions of the female and male reproductive systems; it also plays a role in controlling several aspects of human behavior.

23. **Pathological Liar**: A person who is obsessed with lying about things, sometimes for personal gain or even without any personal benefits. These people can even harm themselves.

24. **Procreation**: The process or act of getting one's offspring.

25. **Red Flags**: The prominent signs in a person that exhibits manipulative, dangerous, and unhealthy behaviors.

26. **Rekindle**: To revive or start up all over again; to reignite love between couples, especially in a married or dating relationship after a severe fight or breakup.

27. **Rubbing Salt in the Wound**: When someone tries to convert a difficult and bad situation into an even worse one.

28. **Silhouette**: Showing an outline or profile of someone, especially on a light background with shadows around their image.

29. **Sociopath**: A psychological or mental condition in which a person shows consistent selfish behavior with no sense of right and wrong, a lack of empathy for others, lying for personal benefits, using violence, and impulsive behaviors.

30. **Spiritual Meditation**: A meditation technique that helps you understand your inner self, or the core, which supports you in finding peace and tranquility.

31. **Stone Walling**: Showing an extreme gesture of non-cooperation and not complying with

others; in a married relationship, it means to be inaccessible or unavailable emotionally for your spouse.

32. **Tarot Cards**: A card used by practitioners to explore and look into the past, present, and future of a person.

33. **Through Thick and Thin**: Being with someone in all situations, be it good, bad, or worse.

34. **Voodoo**: Someone who can deal with magic or spells; a religion that is followed in Africa that includes magical practices as a part of their religious rituals.

35. **Yin and Yang**: A description of the philosophical concept in Chinese culture that depicts the existence of opposite energies that are interrelated with each other.

References

Aries, E. (2016, May 12). *How a toxic relationship can ruin your career*. Medium. https://medium.com/@BossedUpOrg/how-a-toxic-relationship-can-ruin-your-career-a797d77b97db

Basile, L. M. (2016, July 23). *10 signs a marriage is doomed*. Red Book. https://www.redbookmag.com/life/news/g3545/divorce-signs-marriage/

Bhandari, S. (2022, December 13). *Recovering from trauma*. WebMD. https://www.webmd.com/mental-health/ss/slideshow-emotional-trauma-self-care

Brady, K. (2021, May 19). *7 tips for repairing your relationship after a fight*. Keir Brady Counseling Services. https://keirbradycounseling.com/7-tips-for-repairing-your-relationship-after-a-fight/

Buffalmano, L. (2018, September 4). *11 types of toxic relationships*. Power Dynamics. https://thepowermoves.com/toxic-relationships/

Campbell, K. (2017, October 24). *5 warning signs of a doomed marriage*. Bay View Therapy. https://www.bayviewtherapy.com/single-post/5-warning-signs-of-a-doomed-marriage

Chamlou, N. (2022, August 19). *How to rekindle a relationship: 7 ways to ignite the spark*. Psych Central. https://psychcentral.com/relationships/how-to-rekindle-a-relationship

Cherry, K. (2018). *Understanding factors and behaviors that predict domestic violence*. Verywell Mind. https://www.verywellmind.com/signs-that-a-relationship-could-turn-violent-4100203

Claery, & Hammond. (2021, April 23). *10 signs that it's time to divorce*. Claery & Hammond, LLP. https://www.claerygreen.com/family-law-blog/2021/april/10-signs-that-its-time-to-divorce/

Codependent Quotes. (2022, September 11). *Best +35 codependency quotes every codependent needs to read.* Ineffable Living. https://ineffableliving.com/codependency-quotes/

Coppa, C. (2015, December 23). *9 important signs your marriage can be saved.* Woman's Day. https://www.womansday.com/relationships/dating-marriage/g2074/how-to-save-your-marriage/

Elitou, H. (2022, April 4). *Will Smith and Jada Pinkett Smith's relationship timeline.* Brides. https://www.brides.com/will-smith-jada-pinkett-smith-relationship-timeline-5190764#:~:text=The%20couple%20met%20on%20the

Firestone, L. (2013, April 29). *In a relationship with a narcissist? A guide to narcissistic relationships.* Psych Alive. https://www.psychalive.org/narcissistic-relationships/

Gaspard, T. (2016, December 8). *10 ways to rekindle the passion in your marriage.* The Gottman Institute. https://www.gottman.com/blog/10-ways-rekindle-passion-marriage/

Gonzalez, A. (2023, January 6). *Healthy vs. unhealthy relationships.* WebMD. https://www.webmd.com/sex-relationships/healthy-vs-unhealthy-relationships

Gualtieri, J. (2019, March 9). *5 different types of unhealthy relationships.* The Date Mix. https://www.zoosk.com/date-mix/dating-advice/unhealthy-relationships/

Gurung, S. (2022, April 18). *Patrick Dempsey & Jillian Dempsey relationship timeline.* Featured Biography. https://featuredbiography.com/patrick-dempsey-jillian-dempsey-relationship-timeline/

Kenneth, M. (2020, June 8). *These 10 things cause divorce in a marriage.* Show Case City Online. https://medium.com/showcasecityonline/these-10-things-cause-divorce-in-a-marriage-8a9f5a4f2979

Khan, S. (2018, April 19). *5 ways toxic relationships affect your physical health.* News 18. https://www.news18.com/news/indiwo/parenting-and-family-5-ways-toxic-relationships-affect-your-physical-health-1722949.html

Kreienberg, M. (2022, July 29). *Kristen Bell and Dax Shepard's relationship timeline.* Brides. https://www.brides.com/kristen-bell-dax-shepard-relationship-timeline-5100885#:~:text=Kristen%20Bell%20and%20Dax%20Shepard%20met%20at%20a%20dinner%20party

Lamothe, C., & Raypole, C. (2022, January 11). *What is a toxic relationship? 14 signs and what to do.* Healthline. https://www.healthline.com/health/toxic-relationship#What-is-a-toxic-relationship?

Lutkin, A. (2023, March 25). *Jessica Biel and Justin Timberlake enjoy a night out at SZA's concert.* ELLE. https://www.elle.com/culture/celebrities/a43102874/jessica-biel-justin-timberlake-relationship-timeline/

Manson, M. (2019, January 14). *3 core components of a healthy relationship.* Mark Manson. https://markmanson.net/3-core-components-of-a-healthy-relationship#:~:text=All%20healthy%20relationships%20share%20the

Mendelsohn, H. (2022, September 21). *Expert-backed solutions to an emotionally abusive relationship.* Brides. https://www.brides.com/signs-of-an-emotionally-abusive-relationship-5112027

Miguel, M. (2022, February 9). *Many people find themselves with a sociopath, so it's important to be able to recognize the signs of sociopathy in your relationship.* We Heart. https://www.we-heart.com/2022/02/09/15-signs-of-sociopathy-in-your-relationship/

Omogbolagun, T. (2022, January 15). *When your partner is carefree.* Punch Newspapers. https://punchng.com/when-your-partner-is-carefree/

Pace, R. (2021, October 18). *11 types of bad relationships you need to get out of right now.* Marriage Advice - Expert Marriage Tips & Advice. https://www.marriage.com/advice/relationship/types-of-bad-relationships-you-need-to-get-out-of-now/

Ralney, D. (2018, January 11). *6 steps for resolving conflict in marriage.* FamilyLife. https://www.familylife.com/articles/topics/

marriage/staying-married/resolving-conflict/6-steps-for-resolving-conflict-in-marriage/

Resnick, A. (2022, February 3). *10 ways to heal from trauma.* Verywell Mind. https://www.verywellmind.com/10-ways-to-heal-from-trauma-5206940

Rukaite, U., & Lyskoit, V. (2022, August 28). *150 toxic relationship quotes to stop hurting yourself and let go.* Bored Panda. https://www.boredpanda.com/toxic-relationship-quotes/?utm_source=google&utm_medium=organic&utm_campaign=organic

Shutterfly Community. (2018, October 29). *45+ marriage quotes for any occasion* Shutterfly. https://www.shutterfly.com/ideas/marriage-quotes/

Smith, S. (2020, December 24). *20 signs you are in a competitive relationship.* Marriage Advice - Expert Marriage Tips & Advice. https://www.marriage.com/advice/relationship/signs-you-are-in-a-competitive-relationship/

Tanney, A. (2015, September 9). *Hazard: 10 types of toxic relationships to avoid getting involved in.* Elite Daily. https://www.elitedaily.com/dating/types-of-toxic-relationships/1170703

Tete, S. (2021, August 5). *Conflict in relationships: Causes & best ways to deal with it.* Style Craze. https://www.stylecraze.com/articles/conflict-in-relationships/

Turecki, J. (2021, June 14). *The differences between healthy, unhealthy and toxic relationships.* Jillian Turecki. https://www.jillianturecki.com/blog/2021/6/14/the-differences-between-healthy-unhealthy-and-toxic-relationships#:~:text=The%20key%20difference%20between%20an

US Weekly Staff. (2022, January 3). *Boat babes! Victoria and David Beckham embrace in sweet new shot.* Us Weekly. https://www.usmagazine.com/celebrity-news/pictures/david-and-victoria-beckhams-relationship-timeline/

About the Author

Joseph Ajayi, a pastor and writer, is unwavering in his commitment to enhancing lives and fostering success in personal and professional spheres. Throughout his career, he has devoted himself to empowering individuals and families, nurturing their growth and well-being. His vision spans numerous focus areas, including self-improvement, relationships, family dynamics, ministry growth, management principles, business intelligence, and leadership development. He holds a bachelor's degree in engineering, a Master of Business Administration (MBA), and a Doctor of Philosophy (Ph.D.) in organizational leadership. He lives in Ramsey, Minnesota, with his wife and three children.

.

Made in the USA
Monee, IL
07 June 2024

59542820R00125